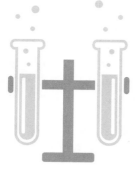

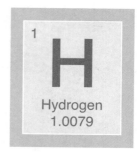

CHEMISTRY

Investigate the Matter That Makes Up Your World

INQUIRE AND INVESTIGATE

Carla Mooney
Illustrated by Samuel Carbaugh

Nomad Press
A division of Nomad Communications
10 9 8 7 6 5 4 3 2 1

This book was manufactured by Marquis Book Printing,
Montmagny, Québec, Canada
May 2016, Job #121611
ISBN Softcover: 978-1-61930-365-2
ISBN Hardcover: 978-1-61930-361-4

Educational Consultant, Marla Conn

Questions regarding the ordering of this book should be addressed to
Nomad Press
2456 Christian St.
White River Junction, VT 05001
www.nomadpress.net

Printed in Canada.

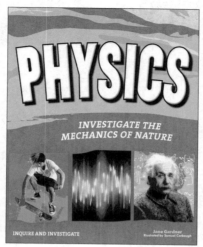

Science titles in the
Inquire and Investigate series

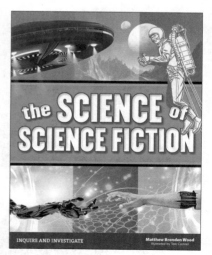

You can use a smartphone or tablet app to scan
the QR codes and explore more about chemistry!
Cover up neighboring QR codes to make sure
you're scanning the right one. You can find a
list of each URL on the Resources page.

If the QR code doesn't work, try searching the Internet
with the Keyword Prompts to find other helpful sources.

Contents

Timeline vi

Introduction
Chemistry Matters! 1

Chapter 1
Atoms, Elements, and the Periodic Table 11

Chapter 2
States of Matter: Gases, Liquids, and Solids 23

Chapter 3
Changing States of Matter 39

Chapter 4
Compounds, Mixtures, and Solutions 47

Chapter 5
Chemical Reactions 65

Chapter 6
Acids and Bases 81

Chapter 7
The Nucleus and Radioactivity 91

Chapter 8
Other Branches of Chemistry 101

Glossary ▾ **Metric Conversions** ▾ **Resources** ▾ **Periodic Table** ▾ **Index**

TIMELINE

460 BCE–370 BCE ...... Democritus of ancient Greece introduces the idea of matter in the form of particles, which he calls atoms. He proposes that all matter is made up of these tiny units.

300 BCE .... Aristotle of ancient Greece declares that there are only four elements: fire, air, water, and earth. He believes that all matter is made from these four elements.

300 BCE .... For many centuries, early chemists called alchemists unsuccessfully attempt to change lead and other metals into gold. They are also unsuccessful in attempts to create an elixir of life that would cure all illnesses and enable people to live longer.

1662 .... Sir Robert Boyle develops fundamental gas laws and defines the inverse relationship between pressure and any gas, which would become known as Boyle's law.

1702 .... Georg Stahl names phlogiston, the substance he believes is released during the process of burning.

1754 .... Joseph Black identifies carbon dioxide gas, which he calls "fixed air."

1774 .... Joseph Priestley discovers oxygen, carbon monoxide, and nitrous oxide.

1787 .... Antoine Laurent Lavoisier publishes his system for classifying and naming chemical substances. He is later known as the father of chemistry.

1803 .... John Dalton develops a theory that matter is made of atoms of different weights and is combined in ratios by weight. He also proposes that atoms are spherical and are in motion.

1809 .... Joseph Louis Gay-Lussac shows that when gases combine, they do so in simple ratios by volume, which is later known as his law of combining volumes.

1828 .... Friedrich Wöhler synthesizes urea, proving that organic compounds can be produced from inorganic materials.

1865 .... Johann Josef Loschmidt determines the exact number of molecules in a mole, later called Avogadro's number.

1869 .... Dmitri Mendeleev publishes the first modern periodic table to classify elements. The table allows scientists to predict the properties of undiscovered elements.

1884 .... Henry Louis Le Chatelier develops Le Chatelier's principle to explain how chemical equilibrium responds to external stresses.

1898	J.J. Thomson discovers the electron.
1898	Marie Curie and her husband, Pierre, isolate the element radium. Because they do not know about the danger of radioactivity, they work without any protection.
1900	Ernest Rutherford discovers that decaying atoms create radioactivity.
1906	Frederick Soddy observes chemically identical elements with different atomic weights and names them isotopes.
1908	Robert Millikan measures the charge of a single electron.
1909	S.P.L. Sorensen invents the idea of pH and develops methods for measuring acidity.
1911	Ernest Rutherford, Hans Geiger, and Ernest Marsden prove the nuclear model of the atom, which has a small, dense, positively charged nucleus surrounded by an electron cloud.
1913	Niels Bohr proposes the Bohr atomic model. His model shows electrons traveling in orbits around an atom's nucleus. Bohr proposes that an atom's chemical properties are determined by how many electrons are in its outer orbits.
1932	James Chadwick discovers the neutron.
1936	Scientists confirm the creation of the first synthetic element, technetium.
1938	Otto Hahn discovers the process of nuclear fission.
1939	Linus Pauling publishes his work on chemical bonds.
1949	Willard Libby develops radiocarbon dating.
1965	Robert Woodward wins the Nobel Prize for his syntheses of compounds such as cholesterol, quinine, chlorophyll, and cobalamin.
2014	Scientists report that acid rain has changed the water chemistry of many of Canada's lakes, which has led to an increase in a tiny plankton coated in gel. Increased numbers of these tiny organisms make the lakes appear as if they have transformed into "jelly."
2015	Chemists successfully use synthetic nanoparticles to deliver therapies to the livers of patients with liver cancer. The therapies suppress their tumors.

Introduction ▶

Chemistry Matters!

What is chemistry and what does it have to do with the world around you?

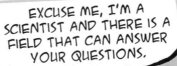

Chemistry is the study of matter that makes up the world around you and the changes that can happen to matter. Matter is anything that has mass and takes up space, including you.

Have you ever wondered what the world is made of? What is the difference between a gas and a liquid? Why does ice melt into water? What happens when something burns? What happens when you mix two substances together? The answers to those questions can all be found in chemistry.

Many people think of chemistry as scientists in white coats mixing strange liquids in a laboratory. They imagine chemists working with molecules, test tubes, and the periodic table. In reality, chemistry is not stuck in a science lab. Chemistry is everywhere. Everything you see, hear, taste, smell, and touch involves chemistry. Chemistry is part of everything you do, from growing and cooking food to cleaning your house to launching a rocket. Learning chemistry can help us understand the world around us.

[Throughout history, humans have enlisted chemistry to make the things we want and need.]

WHAT IS CHEMISTRY?

Chemistry is the study of matter and the changes it undergoes. Matter is anything that has mass and takes up space. Everything on the earth, in the solar system, and in the galaxy is made of matter. It is all of the stuff around you, including your own body. This book is made of matter. Your desk is made of matter. The air you breathe and the water you drink and the food you eat are made of matter.

Matter can exist in different states—solid, liquid, and gas—and it can change back and forth between these states. That's why water can freeze into solid ice, melt into liquid water, and evaporate into water vapor, which is a gas.

Chemists study the properties and the physical and chemical changes of matter. They also study atoms and molecules and the interactions between them. Atoms and molecules are the basic building blocks of matter.

Chemistry is a physical science. It is also known as the central science, because it affects all other natural sciences, including physics, biology, and geology. Everything in the universe is made of matter, which is why chemistry interacts with other sciences so often. Scientists working in other fields often study chemistry to better understand their own areas.

Even before it was defined as a science, chemistry was used by people. For thousands of years, people have been fermenting food and extracting metal from ores, both of which use chemistry. Making glass and soap, using plants to make medicines, and creating pottery also use chemistry.

VOCAB LAB

There is a lot of new vocabulary in this book! Turn to the glossary in the back when you come to a word you don't understand. Practice your new vocabulary in the **VOCAB LAB** activities in each chapter.

CHEMISTRY CONNECTION

Being able to measure accurately is the first step in understanding chemistry. You'll need to be able to use the metric system and also know which numbers are important and which are not.

Today, scientists are using chemistry to improve our daily lives even more. Through chemistry, we can make products such as food, clothing, and construction materials even better. Chemists are also working to protect the environment, improve agriculture, and find new sources of energy.

MEASUREMENTS IN CHEMISTRY

We use measurements every day. Many times, it is simple to find and understand measurements. If someone asks you how long your desk is, you can use a ruler and measure it to the closest inch. Want to find out how much you weigh? It's easy to step on a scale to see how many pounds you are. When the thermometer outside shows that the temperature has dropped to 50 degrees Fahrenheit, you know that it's chilly enough for a jacket!

In chemistry, measurements are a bit different. Scientists use a system of measurement called the metric system. Instead of using inches and pounds, you'll work with centimeters, kilograms, and degrees Celsius.

The metric system is based on seven base units of measurement.

UNIT	QUANTITY	SYMBOL
meter	length or distance	m
kilogram	mass	kg
second	time	s
ampere	electrical current	A
kelvin	temperature	K
mole	quantity of substance	mol
candela	luminous intensity	cd

The metric system adds prefixes to these base units that can be used to measure something very small or very large. For example, it would not make sense to measure the driving distance between New York City and San Francisco in meters because the number would be extremely large!

By adding the prefix "kilo," you can measure the distance between the two cities in kilometers. One kilometer equals 1,000 meters and is a more appropriate measurement for long distances. Instead of saying that you have to drive 4,280,000 meters, you can say that you will drive 4,280 kilometers.

> The metric system's prefixes allow you to convert a big quantity to a smaller quantity by simply moving a decimal point.

Here are some of the most common prefixes in the metric system.

PREFIX	CONVERSION	SYMBOL
giga	1,000,000,000	G
mega	1,000,000	M
kilo	1,000	k
deca	10	da
deci	0.1	d
centi	0.01	c
milli	0.001	m
micro	0.000001	µ

CHEMISTRY CONNECTION

A box of cereal might say that it contains approximately 481 grams. Depending on the scale used to measure the cereal, a specific box may hold 475 grams, 483 grams, or 490 grams of cereal. All non-count measurements have some degree of uncertainty.

Significant figures are the number of digits in a measured or calculated number that gives meaningful information about what is being measured or calculated. They tell other scientists about the quality of data and measurements.

Some measurements, such as counts, are exact. If you count the number of dice in a cup, you know exactly how many dice there are. Other measurements are not so easy. To determine how many significant figures are in a measurement, scientists follow these general rules.

- All nonzero digits are significant. If the mass of a pencil is recorded at 5.23 grams, all three digits are significant.

- Zeros between nonzero digits are significant. If the mass of the pencil is 5.04 grams, all three digits are significant.

- All zeros to the left of the nonzero digits are never significant. If the mass of a staple is 0.0014 grams, only the 1 and the 4 are significant. The zeros to the left of these numbers are not significant figures. If you originally found a measurement to be 1.4 milligrams and then converted that to 0.0014 grams, the quality of your measurement did not change when you converted units, so the number of significant figures should also not change.

- Zeros to the right of the nonzero digits are only significant if there is a decimal point shown. For example, if the mass of an apple is 100.0 grams, all four digits are significant. On the other hand, if the mass of an apple is reported as 100 grams, only the 1 is significant, because it is possible that the measurement was rounded to the nearest 100 grams.

The activities in *Chemistry: Investigate the Matter That Makes Up Your World* will introduce you to the concepts that are used to explain matter and the changes it undergoes. Chemistry is all around us. Are you ready to use chemistry to better understand your world?

KEY QUESTIONS

- **Why does the study of chemistry affect so many other fields of science?**
- **How has chemistry improved your life?**

SIGNIFICANT FIGURES IN A CALCULATION

When using significant figures in a calculation, you will first need to determine the number of significant figures in the data used in the calculation. Then, the answer should be written in the smallest number of significant figures. For example, if a calculation uses one piece of data with three significant figures and another with four significant figures, the answer should be written in three significant figures.

Research significant figures and how they are used in chemistry. You can get started with these websites.

 significant figures

CONVERTING UNITS

Chemistry uses many types of measurements. Some of the most common include distance, mass, time, temperature, volume, density, pressure, amount, concentration, energy, velocity, molarity, viscosity, and electric charge. Each of these can be measured in different ways. For example, mass can be measured in pounds, ounces, grams, and kilograms. Because of these differences, chemists must know how to convert measured quantities into metric units.

The factor-label method allows you to easily convert units from one type of unit to another. All you need is a conversion factor!

- **A conversion factor is a number that lets you convert one set of units to another.** For example, let's convert a dog's weight of 25 pounds to kilograms.

    1. To solve this problem, set up the following equation:

    $$25 \text{ pounds} \times \frac{}{} =$$

    2. Next, write the unit that you already know below the line:

    $$25 \text{ pounds} \times \frac{}{\text{pounds}} =$$

    3. Then, write the unit that you are converting to above the line:

    $$25 \text{ pounds} \times \frac{\text{kilograms}}{\text{pounds}} =$$

4. Now, this is where you need to know the conversion factor. There are 2.21 pounds in 1 kilogram. Add this to the equation:

$$25 \text{ pounds} \times \frac{1 \text{ kilogram}}{2.21 \text{ pounds}} =$$

5. Solve the equation. The pounds cancel each other out, leaving kilogram as the unit.

$$25 \cancel{\text{ pounds}} \times \frac{1 \text{ kilogram}}{2.21 \cancel{\text{ pounds}}} = \qquad 25 \times \frac{1}{2.21} = 11.3 \text{ kilograms}$$

- **Some unit conversion problems are not so simple.** You may need to perform several steps to convert from one unit to another. You can still use the same factor-label method to do the conversion. For example, let's assume that you want to convert 30 miles to meters. You know that there are 1.6 kilometers in 1 mile.

1. To set up a multi-step conversion problem, start with the unit that you are trying to convert:

$$30 \text{ miles} \times \text{———} =$$

2. Next, write the unit that you already know below the line:

$$30 \text{ miles} \times \frac{\text{———}}{\text{miles}} =$$

3. Just like the simple unit conversion problem, add the conversion factor that you know to the equation:

$$30 \text{ miles} \times \frac{1.6 \text{ kilometers}}{1 \text{ miles}} =$$

Inquire & Investigate

CONVERSION FACTORS

You can find conversion factors here to help you convert any measurement into the metric system.

🔍 metric conversion factors

This project continues on the next page. - - - →

Inquire & Investigate

4. Solve the first step of the conversion problem, remembering that the miles cross each other out, leaving kilometers as the units for the answer:

$$30 \cancel{\text{ miles }} \times \frac{1.6 \text{ kilometers}}{1 \cancel{\text{ miles}}} = \quad 30 \times \frac{1.6}{1} = 48 \text{ kilometers}$$

5. You've got the answer in kilometers—48. That's not what you wanted, however. You need to find the answer in meters. So you've got another conversion to do! You know that there are 1,000 meters in a kilometer.

$$48 \cancel{\text{ kilometers}} \times \frac{1,000 \text{ meters}}{1 \cancel{\text{ kilometer}}} = 48,000 \text{ meters}$$

6. You've calculated 30 miles = 48,000 meters!

- **Knowing how to convert unit measurements is a skill that chemists rely on every day.** Now it's your turn to practice your conversion skills! Use the factor-label method to solve the following problems. Remember, you may need to perform multi-step conversions to find the answers!

1. Find the number of seconds in the month of October.

2. Convert 170 pounds to kilograms. There are 2.21 pounds in one kilogram.

3. The Empire State Building is 1,454 feet tall. How tall is it in meters?

4. How many cookies can you buy if you have $23 and they cost $3 per dozen?

5. A painter is painting a fence that measures 400 meters long and 2 meters high. Paint costs $17 per gallon. If a gallon of paint covers 50 square meters, how much paint will the painter need? How much will it cost to paint the fence?

Check your answers in the resources in the back of this book.

Chapter 1
Atoms, Elements, and the Periodic Table

THE FIRST THING YOU MUST KNOW, IS THAT **EVERYTHING YOU SEE** IS MADE OF WHAT YOU CAN'T SEE—ATOMS!

How are atoms, elements, and the periodic table related to each other?

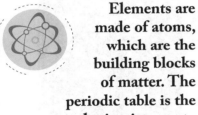
Elements are made of atoms, which are the building blocks of matter. The periodic table is the tool scientists use to organize the different elements according to their properties.

Everything around you is made of matter. But what is matter made of? Matter consists of tiny building blocks called atoms. Atoms can be densely packed together to form a solid object, such as this book. Or atoms can be more spread out and appear as a liquid or a gas. Understanding atoms and how they work is at the heart of chemistry.

PARTS OF AN ATOM

Atoms contain three basic parts—protons, neutrons, and electrons. Protons and neutrons exist inside the nucleus of the atom, which is the center of the atom. Electrons stay outside the nucleus.

Protons are small particles with positive electrical charges, represented by the plus symbol (+). The number of protons in an atom determines what element it is. For example, an atom with two protons is always an element called helium, while an atom with six protons is an element called carbon.

Neutrons, unlike protons, have no electrical charge. A neutron's job is to help stabilize the atom. To understand why, think about two magnets and their poles, or ends. If the poles have opposite charges, which means one is positive while the other is negative, they attract each other and pull together. But if the poles have the same charge, both positive or both negative, they repel and push away from each other.

In the same way, protons with the same positive charge repel each other. Neutrons act like peacemakers, keeping the protons collected together and stabilizing the atom's nucleus.

[Together, an atom's protons and neutrons make up most of its mass.]

Electrons are small, negatively charged particles that exist outside of the atom's nucleus. We use the minus symbol (-) to represent an electron. The opposite charges of the electron and proton attract each other, just as opposite magnetic poles attract each other. This force holds the atom together.

The positive charge of one proton and the negative charge of one electron cancel each other out. Therefore, an atom with the same number of protons and electrons will have no charge and will be neutral.

While the number of protons in an atom does not change, some special atoms can have more or fewer electrons. These are called ions. An atom that gains electrons becomes negatively charged and is called an anion. An atom that loses electrons becomes positively charged and is called a cation. The "t" in the word *cation* makes a plus sign to remind us it's positive.

Electrons are very small compared to the rest of the atom. In fact, the mass of an electron is more than 1,000 times smaller than the mass of a proton.

STICKY ATOMS

Have you ever rubbed a balloon against your head and had it stay there even after you let it go? Static electricity happens because electrons and protons attract and repel each other. When you rub that balloon on your head, electrons transfer from your head to the balloon. The balloon now has more electrons than protons, giving it a negative charge. Your head has lost some electrons, giving it a positive charge. The negatively charged balloon is attracted to the positive charge on your head. Try it!

ATOMIC ORBITALS

So where exactly are an atom's electrons? The answer is actually pretty complicated. Electrons are always moving, spinning in clouds around the atom's nucleus. Because electrons move so quickly, chemists cannot see where they are at any specific moment. Scientists used to believe that electrons orbited the nucleus of an atom like planets around the sun. With more research, they discovered that this idea was too simple.

Chemists now believe that there are specific areas where electrons are likely to be found. An atom's electrons are located in energy levels, numbered 1, 2, 3, and so on. Energy levels are different distances from the atom's nucleus. Energy level 1 is the closest to the nucleus, while the highest number energy level is the farthest away. An electron spinning in the first energy level will always be closer to the nucleus than an electron spinning in the second energy level. The more electrons an atom has, the more energy levels it has.

Inside each energy level, there are spaces where electrons are likely to be located. These spaces are called orbitals. Chemists have named electron orbitals with letters, such as s, p, d, f, and g.

ATOMS HAVE ELECTRONS ORBITING THE NUCLEUS. RIGHT, PROF?

THAT'S RIGHT! DIFFERENT ATOMS HAVE DIFFERENT ENERGY LEVELS BASED ON THE POSITION OF THE ELECTRONS.

LEVEL 1   LEVEL 2   LEVEL 3

Orbitals are different shapes. For example, the s orbital is shaped like a sphere, while the p orbital is shaped like a dumbbell.

Electrons usually fill the lowest energy levels first. If electrons were filling a theater to see a performance, they would all take seats in the front row until it was full, then move on to the second row, and so on. There is a limit to the number of electrons that can inhabit each energy level. The first energy level holds up to two electrons, and the second energy level can hold up to eight electrons.

The formula $2 \times n^2$, where n = the energy level, can be used to figure out how many electrons each energy level can hold. Using this formula, we know that the third energy level can hold up to 18 electrons ($2 \times 3^2 = 18$).

WHAT IS AN ELEMENT?

Thousands of years ago, ancient Greek philosophers believed that all matter was made from combinations of just four elements—earth, water, air, and fire. Although we know today that they were wrong, the idea that elements are the basis of all matter is actually true.

An element is something that cannot be broken down into a simpler substance. It is something that is made up of only one type of atom. To date, scientists have discovered 118 different elements. These 118 elements combine to make millions of different substances.

Some elements, such as gold, copper, and carbon, have been known for thousands of years. Others, such as livermorium, have been discovered recently. In the future, even more elements might be discovered.

To describe the electrons in an atom, scientists use a notation called an electron configuration:

n (type of orbital) number of electrons

A hydrogen atom has only one electron, which can be found in the first energy level (1), in the s orbital. Its electron configuration can be written as $1s^1$ and looks like this:

The atom beryllium has four electrons, two in the first energy level and two in the second. Therefore, beryllium's electron configuration is $1s^2 \, 2s^2$. It looks like this:

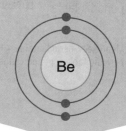

THE PERIODIC TABLE

The atoms that make up all known elements are organized on a chart called the periodic table of elements. It is organized in a grid, with rows and columns. You can use the large periodic table on page 117 as a reference for the rest of the book.

Each element on the periodic table is located in a specific square based on its atomic structure and characteristics. Each square displays certain information about that element, including its element name, symbol, atomic number, and atomic mass. Every element is represented by one or two letters called its atomic symbol. For example, the element lithium's atomic symbol is Li, while the element carbon's atomic symbol is C. Iron is Fe.

Every element also has an atomic number. For example, lithium's atomic number is 3. Carbon's is 6.

The periodic table lists elements in the order of their atomic number, from left to right and top to bottom. An element's atomic number tells you how many protons are in that atom's nucleus. In a lithium atom, which has an atomic number of 3, there are three protons. In a carbon atom, there are six protons. Because neutral atoms have the same number of protons and electrons, an element's atomic number can also tell you how many electrons it has. Therefore, a lithium atom also has three electrons and a carbon atom has six electrons.

Each square on the periodic table also shows the element's average atomic mass. Elements are so tiny that it does not make sense to measure them in kilograms or even grams. Scientists use a unit of measurement called an amu (atomic mass unit) to measure the mass of an atom.

HISTORY OF THE PERIODIC TABLE

In 1869, a Russian chemist named Dmitri Mendeleev was the first to publish a periodic table similar to the one we use today. It's said that he used to play a kind of solitaire on long train rides using cards with information about the elements written out on them. This helped him figure out how to group the elements together in a chart.

You can see Mendeleev's original table here.

You can see an interactive version of the periodic table we use today here.

Watch videos about every element in the periodic table!

Mendeleev periodic table · PBS periodic table · periodic videos

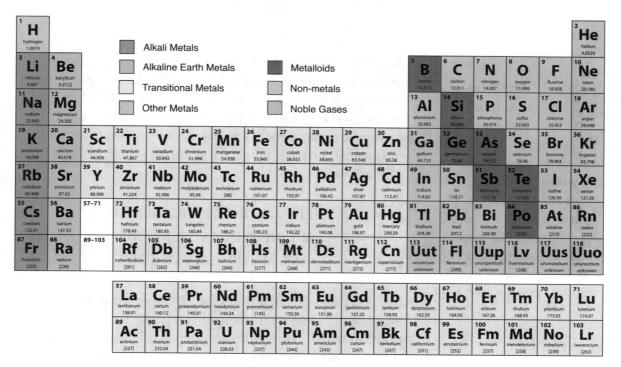

Use the larger periodic table on page 117 for reference.

CHEMISTRY CONNECTION

Atoms in the same vertical column on the periodic table have the same number of electrons in the outermost energy level. These electrons are called valence electrons. Valence electrons interact with other atoms and give the atom many of its properties.

Elements on the periodic table are organized into rows and columns. Each row is called a period. Every element in a row has the same number of atomic energy levels. For example, every element on the table's top row has one energy level. As you move down the table, each row adds another energy level. Elements in the second row have two energy levels, while elements in the third row have three energy levels, and so on.

The columns are called groups, or families. The groups are numbered from 1 to 18, left to right. Elements in the same group have similar chemical properties, but different physical properties.

The elements in group 2 are alkaline earth metals. These are shiny and silvery white in color. Other groups include noble gases (group 18), alkali metals (group 1), halogens (group 17), and transitional metals (groups 3 to 12).

CHEMISTRY CONNECTION

Because an element can have different isotopes, the mass on the periodic table is actually the average atomic mass of the element. This number is calculated using a weighted average of all the masses of all the isotopes of an element.

An element's place on the periodic table can also give information about its electron configuration, or where the atom's electrons are located in orbitals. Elements in the same column have the same valence electron configurations, which are the electrons in the atom's outermost energy level. As a result, they behave in similar ways.

[
With this knowledge, chemists can predict how atoms will react in different situations.
]

By using the periodic table, you can learn a lot about an element. For example, nitrogen (N) has an atomic number of 7. This number tells you that a neutral nitrogen atom has seven protons and seven electrons.

Because nitrogen is in the second row or period of the table, its electrons can be found in two energy levels. You know that the first energy level contains two electrons. Putting it together, you can figure out that a nitrogen atom has two electrons in the first energy level and five electrons in the second energy level.

METALS, NONMETALS, AND METALLOIDS

On the periodic table, there is a line that starts in front of the element boron (B) and steps down the table and ends between polonium (Po) and astatine (At). This line separates metals and nonmetals. Elements that are metals are located on the left of the line, while nonmetals are found on the right.

Some elements do not fit neatly into metal or nonmetal categories and have properties of both. These elements are called metalloids. They include boron, silicon, germanium, arsenic, antimony, tellurium, and polonium. On the periodic table, these elements are placed directly next to the dividing line between metals and nonmetals.

ISOTOPES OF AN ELEMENT

In some cases, atoms of an element might be slightly different. They might weigh different amounts. How does this happen if all the atoms of an element have the same number of protons?

Remember the neutrons in the atom's nucleus? While the number of protons cannot change, atoms of the same element can have a different number of neutrons. When this happens, the atom's atomic mass is changed. Atoms of the same element with different atomic masses are called isotopes.

THE ATOMIC MAKEUP OF THINGS IS REALLY IMPORTANT.

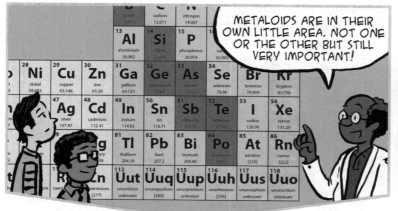

METALOIDS ARE IN THEIR OWN LITTLE AREA, NOT ONE OR THE OTHER BUT STILL VERY IMPORTANT!

I GUESS THE PROF IS RIGHT, NOTHING IS TOO SMALL TO *MATTER!*

For example, the element lithium has three protons in its nucleus. These positively charged protons are separated and stabilized by either three or four neutrons. Depending on whether the atom has three or four neutrons, it will weigh different amounts. These two atoms—with either three or four neutrons—are isotopes of lithium.

VALENCE ELECTRONS AND THE OCTET RULE

Atoms like to be stable. Stability requires less energy. As with everything in the nature, atoms try to do the most work with the least amount of effort.

A stable atom has a complete outer energy level. The electrons in the atom's outer energy level are called valence electrons. The number of valence electrons determines the properties of the element.

The octet rule in chemistry says that atoms are most stable when they have full outer energy levels, complete with eight electrons. Sometimes, an atom will have more or less than eight valence electrons. They will try to gain or lose valence electrons in order to reach their goal of eight. They can gain or lose electrons by bonding with other atoms, either of the same element or with different elements.

Hydrogen (H) and helium (He) are the exceptions to the octet rule. These two elements are perfectly happy with only two electrons in their outer energy levels.

KEY QUESTIONS

- What are the main parts of an atom? What role does each part have?

- Which elements do you come in contact with on a daily basis? What do you use them for?

- Why is the periodic table useful? Would you group the elements in different ways?

THREE-DIMENSIONAL ATOM

Atoms can be broken down into three basic parts—protons, neutrons, and electrons. Using a few common household items, you can build three-dimensional models of different types of atoms.

Ideas for Supplies ▼

- small sticker dots
- variety of different colored gumdrops
- several wooden toothpicks
- several long wooden skewers
- periodic table (page 117)

- **Label the sticker dots with symbols to represent the electrical charge.** A plus symbol (+) represents a positive charge, a zero (0) is neutral, and a minus symbol (-) is a negative charge.

- **Select gumdrops to represent protons, neutrons, and electrons.** Label each with the appropriate sticker dot.

- **Using the toothpicks, create a nucleus containing protons and neutrons for a lithium atom.** You may need to break the toothpicks into pieces. Use the periodic table to figure out how many protons and neutrons are in a lithium atom.

- **Attach electrons to your lithium atom's nucleus.** Use the long wooden skewers.

- **What charge does the atom have?** Why? If you remove one electron, what charge does it now have? Why?

- **Using the periodic table, select several other atoms, such as helium, carbon, and oxygen.** Create models for these atoms.

> **To investigate more, try combining several atom models to create molecules. Ideas include water (H$_2$O) and carbon dioxide (CO$_2$).**

HMMM...I WONDER IF I HAVE ENOUGH GUM DROPS LEFT TO MAKE RADIUM? YUMMY YUMMY RADIUM!

Inquire & Investigate

VOCAB LAB

Write down what you think each word means:

electron, proton, neutron, orbital, valence electrons, element, metalloid, isotope, octet rule, and **ion**.

Discuss your definitions with friends using real-life examples. Did you all come up with the same definitions? Turn to the text and the glossary if you need help.

USING THE PERIODIC TABLE

The periodic table has several pieces of information about the atoms of the elements. In this activity, you will use the periodic table to investigate different elements.

Using a periodic table, answer the following questions.

1. What element has eight protons?
2. What is the atomic mass of magnesium?
3. How many electrons does an aluminum atom have?
4. What is the chemical symbol for silver?
5. How many elements are metalloids? How many are nonmetals?
6. What is the atomic number of iron?
7. How many protons, neutrons, and electrons does one atom of calcium have?
8. What is the atomic number of chromium?
9. Which element has an atomic mass of 65.38?
10. How many protons, neutrons, and electrons does the element sodium have?

> To investigate more, select a few elements on the periodic table to research. How are they alike and how are they different? How does the periodic table give you information about the physical and chemical properties of these elements?

Check your answers in the resources in the back of this book.

Chapter 2
States of Matter: Gases, Liquids, and Solids

MATTER COMES IN DIFFERENT STATES. YOUR SODA HAS TWO COMBINED.

SODA

What is different about the different forms of matter?

In a solid, molecules are bound closely together. In a liquid, molecules are able to move away from each other more. In a gas, molecules move much farther away.

Everything around us is made of matter, but not everything has the same characteristics. Your glass of water is different from your sandwich, and both of these are different from the air you breathe, even though all these things are made of matter.

Some objects are solid, others are liquid, and others are gas. These different forms of matter are called states. Why does matter have different states? What makes some matter a solid, while other matter is a liquid or a gas? The answer can be found with the smallest piece of matter—the atom.

Each form of matter is made up of individual atoms or small groups of atoms bonded together in clusters called molecules. These atoms are always in motion. At the same time, the atoms are attracted to one another because of their charges, as we learned in the last chapter. Together, these two ideas help explain the different states of matter. They are known as the kinetic molecular theory of matter.

HARD AS A ROCK—SOLIDS

Some matter is solid, such as a bicycle, ball, and even your own body. Solid matter can have many different physical characteristics. Think of all the different solids you come in contact with every day. A solid can be as hard as a rock or as soft as a kitten's fur. It can be as big as a city skyscraper or as small as a grain of salt.

Although they can look very different, solids have some important similarities. All solids have a fixed shape and a fixed volume. Solids hold their shapes because their atoms and molecules are tightly packed together. In a solid, the molecules are very attracted to each other. This strong attraction keeps the molecules held tightly together in a specific structure or arrangement. The molecules in a solid can only vibrate in place. They cannot move past each other or change their positions.

In some solids, atoms and molecules are arranged in rigid groups called crystals. The crystals are stacked in a repeating, three-dimensional pattern called a crystal lattice. Table salt (NaCl) is an example of a common crystal. In table salt, the sodium (Na) and chlorine (Cl) atoms line up in a specific pattern to form the salt's crystals. There are many different types of crystal structures.

A grain of salt will always look like a grain of salt unless something happens to it. A rock does not spontaneously change its shape. Neither will it flow like a liquid.

CHEMISTRY CONNECTION

The atoms or molecules in a solid are locked into place by chemical bonds or intermolecular forces. The solid's properties often depend on the type of bond or force holding its atoms in place.

SOME SOLIDS, SUCH AS TABLE SALT, HAVE CRYSTAL LATTICES OF PARTICLES THAT INTERLOCK.

WOW! SALT IS ACTUALLY KIND OF BEAUTIFUL!

SALT

GO WITH THE FLOW–LIQUIDS

Anyone who has spilled a can of soda knows that a liquid is very different from a solid! A liquid is fluid, and in the case of soda, sticky. Water, coffee, alcohol, gasoline, and blood are all types of liquids.

Liquids have several common characteristics. Unlike solids, they do not hold their shape. Instead, they fill the shape of the container they are in. If you pour water into a tall glass, it will have a different shape than if you pour it into a shallow bowl. Even though the liquid changes its shape, its volume remains the same no matter what container you use. Also, the top of a liquid is usually a relatively flat surface. This is because the force of gravity pulls on the liquid's molecules and flattens its surface.

Liquids are also difficult to compress. When something is compressed, its molecules are forced into a smaller space. Just as in a solid, the molecules in a liquid are already closely packed together, which makes it hard to compress them any more.

The molecules in a liquid are constantly in motion. The attractions between the liquid's molecules are not as strong as they are in a solid. While a liquid's attractions keep the molecules close to each other, they are not in a fixed position. This allows a liquid's molecules to move past each other.

[The movement of molecules explains why a liquid can easily change its shape.]

Although a liquid's molecules can move freely past one another, they still tend to keep near one another. Liquids often stick together because of forces that pull the molecules together. A drop of water on the floor will tend to stay in a drop instead of spreading out into a large, thin puddle. The intermolecular forces that attract the water molecules to each other keep the water together as a drop. In contrast, a liquid with weaker intermolecular forces, such as ethyl alcohol, will spread out over a larger area.

Intermolecular forces, or forces between molecules, are found in all substances. Most intermolecular forces bring molecules together, while some forces push them apart. A liquid whose molecules are held together by a strong intermolecular force will behave differently from another liquid whose molecules are held together by a weaker intermolecular force. A liquid's intermolecular force affects its melting point, boiling point, and surface tension. The stronger the intermolecular force, the higher the temperature will be at which the liquid will melt and boil.

SURFACE TENSION

Intermolecular forces also affect a liquid's surface tension. Surface tension is that tendency of a liquid to spread in a low surface area. Liquids with stronger intermolecular forces often have higher surface tensions than liquids with weaker intermolecular forces. Water has strong intermolecular forces, while a liquid such as ethyl alcohol has weaker intermolecular forces.

SOME LIQUIDS SEEM TO BE LESS LIQUIDISH THAN OTHERS. ARE THEY "SOLIQUID" OR SOMETHING?

LIQUIDS WITH STRONG FORCES, SUCH AS THOSE IN MERCURY, WILL MAKE THE LIQUID HOLD TOGETHER IN A MORE SOLID-LIKE WAY.

LIQUIDS WITH WEAK FORCES, SUCH AS ETHYL ALCOHOL, SPREAD AND FLOW MORE EASILY. BOTH ARE LIQUID, BUT BEHAVE DIFFERENTLY.

ALL AROUND YOU—GASES

THE FORCE OF PRESSURE

When working with gases, the idea of pressure is important to understand. Pressure is the force exerted by gas particles as they bounce off the sides of the container holding them. In chemistry, there are several common units of pressure—atmospheres (atm), millimeters of mercury (mmHg) or Torr, and pascals (Pa).

CHEMISTRY CONNECTION

An atmosphere is about equal to the pressure the atmosphere is exerting on you. This is assuming you are at sea level and it is not too stormy outside.

Gases are all around you. The earth's atmosphere is made of gases. While solids and liquids are easy to see and touch, gases are often invisible and odorless. They do not have a definite volume or a definite shape.

One of the physical characteristics of a gas is that it can fill a container of any size or shape. Imagine a balloon. Balloons come in all shapes and sizes. Some are round, while others twist and turn to form fancy designs. No matter what size or shape the balloon is, the gas molecules you blow inside will spread out to fill the balloon.

Just as in solids and liquids, the molecules in a gas are constantly moving. Gas molecules vibrate and move freely past each other.

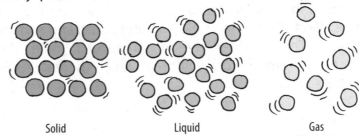

Solid　　　　　Liquid　　　　　Gas

In a gas, the attractions between molecules are much weaker than those in a solid or liquid. As a result, the molecules in a gas spread out much farther than those in liquids and solids. The molecules are so far apart that gases are generally much less dense than liquids or solids. This means gases can be compressed much more easily than solids or liquids. Compressing a gas reduces the space between its molecules.

[Because gas molecules are so spread out, they can mix freely with other gases.]

KINETIC MOLECULAR THEORY OF GASES

Because gases are difficult to see and touch, they can be difficult to study. Scientists have developed some theories to explain the behavior of gases.

One of these theories is kinetic molecular theory (KMT). KMT is a model of gas behavior. It makes the following assumptions about the particles in a gas.

- The particles of a gas are infinitely small.

- The particles of a gas are constantly, randomly moving.

- The molecules of a gas do not experience intermolecular forces.

- The kinetic energy of a gas is proportional to its temperature. The higher the gas's temperature, the faster its particles will move, generating more energy.

- Gas molecules experience perfectly elastic collisions. This means that when they hit each other, they transfer kinetic energy from one to another without any loss of energy.

It is important to understand that the KMT model of gases is not true in the real world. Instead, KMT shows an ideal version of how a gas should behave under perfect conditions. Although an ideal gas does not exist, the KMT model is useful when modeling how real gases behave.

Scientists use the model of an ideal gas to understand why other gases behave the way they do, just as athletes think of the perfect back handspring or the perfect basketball play when they are thinking of ways to improve.

GAS LAWS

OKAY, SO SOLIDS ARE SOLID, LIQUIDS ARE RUNNY, WHAT ABOUT GASES? DO WE KNOW AS MUCH ABOUT THOSE? I MEAN, BESIDES CAUSING SODA TO BLOW UP?

OH YES! THAT'S THE MOST INTERESTING STATE. WELL, THEY ARE ALL INTERESTING, BUT I DO LOVE GAS. THEY'RE SUPER IMPORTANT.

WE INTERACT WITH GASES ALL THE TIME! MOSTLY WE DON'T EVEN NOTICE THEM, BUT WITHOUT GASES, WE WOULDN'T BE ALIVE! WHEW!

Unlike liquids and solids, the volume of a gas is not fixed. A gas can be compressed into a smaller volume by reducing the amount of space between its molecules. Changes in the volume of a gas can affect its pressure. Compressing a gas into a smaller container and a smaller volume causes its molecules to bump into the sides of the container, which increases the pressure of the gas. The volume and pressure of a gas can also be affected by temperature.

Scientists have developed several laws to explain the relationships between the volume, temperature, and pressure of a gas.

Boyle's Law—Volume and Pressure: If the temperature of a gas remains the same, adding pressure will decrease the volume of a gas. This relationship is shown in the following equation:

$$P_1 \times V_1 = P_2 \times V_2$$

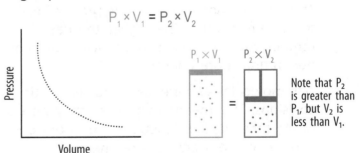

Note that P_2 is greater than P_1, but V_2 is less than V_1.

If the pressure of a gas increases, its volume must decrease proportionally. For example, if the volume of a gas is equal to 2.2 liters at a pressure of 1.3 atm, what happens to the gas when the pressure is decreased to 0.75 atm? You can use the equation to figure it out:

$$1.3 \text{ atm} \times 2.2 \text{ L} = 0.75 \text{ atm} \times V_2$$

$$\frac{1.3 \text{ atm} \times 2.2 \text{ L}}{0.75 \text{ atm}} = \frac{0.75 \text{ atm} \times V_2}{0.75 \text{ atm}}$$

$$3.8 \text{ L} = V_2$$

Charles's Law—Volume and Temperature: If you keep the pressure of a gas the same, increasing its temperature also increases its volume. This occurs because when you increase the temperature of a gas, its molecules move faster and hit the walls of a container with increased energy. The molecules also spread out, increasing its volume as its temperature increases. In order to keep pressure the same, the volume of the gas must increase. This relationship is shown in the following equation:

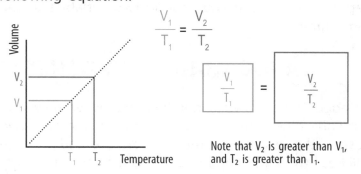

$$\frac{V_1}{T_1} = \frac{V_2}{T_2}$$

$$\boxed{\frac{V_1}{T_1}} = \boxed{\frac{V_2}{T_2}}$$

Note that V_2 is greater than V_1, and T_2 is greater than T_1.

This is a direct relationship, which means that if the temperature increases, the volume of the gas must increase proportionally to help the pressure the same. You can test Charles's law by putting a blown-up balloon in the freezer. Measure it before and after. What happens?

Gay-Lussac's Law—Pressure and Temperature: If the volume of a gas stays the same, increasing temperature increases the pressure of the gas. At a higher temperature, the gas molecules hit the walls of the container with more force, causing pressure to increase. This relationship is shown in the following equation:

$$\frac{P_1}{T_1} = \frac{P_2}{T_2}$$

Note that P_2 is greater than P_1, and T_2 is greater than T_1.

As either pressure or temperature increases, the other also increases. This is why you shouldn't heat a closed container—because it might pop from the pressure.

IDEAL GAS LAW

The ideal gas law explains what happens to an ideal gas if there is a change in pressure, temperature, or volume. It can be written in the following equation:

$$PV = nRT$$

You already know that P, V, and T stand for pressure, volume, and temperature. In this equation, n = the number of moles of gas present and R = the ideal gas constant (0.0821L atm/mol K).

For example, if you have a container full of an ideal gas, the amount of gas molecules is fixed. The gas exerts a pressure on the inside of the container. If you increase the temperature of the gas, the equation tells us that the product of P×V must also increase. If the volume of the container stays the same, then the pressure must increase as a result of the temperature increase.

Systematic error occurs when something goes wrong in an experiment or with a piece of equipment. It causes a scientist to get the same mistake every time the experiment is repeated or data is measured. For example, if a scale is incorrectly balanced to record every weight 25 grams heavier than the objects actually are, it will do this every time it weighs something.

Random error is an error that cannot be explained or reproduced, such as when a scale records three different weights for the same object. Scientists control for random error by making many measurements or repeating an experiment many times. Because scientists know that most experiments have some degree of experimental error, they often assume that the last significant figure in a piece of data is uncertain.

Combined Gas Law: All three of these laws showing the relationship between pressure, temperature, and volume in a gas can be combined into a single equation:

$$\frac{P_1 \times V_1}{T_1} = \frac{P_2 \times V_2}{T_2}$$

Using the combined gas law, you can figure out what happens to a gas if you change two variables at the same time.

AVOGADRO'S HYPOTHESIS

Amedeo Avogadro was an Italian scientist who lived in the early nineteenth century. He discovered that two gases with the same volume, temperature, and pressure will have the same number of molecules. This discovery is known as Avogadro's hypothesis.

Another way of thinking of Avogadro's hypothesis is to picture two identical containers, one containing oxygen gas and the other holding nitrogen gas. If the temperature and pressure are the same, each container will hold the same number of molecules.

But what if different gases have molecules of different sizes? For example, equal numbers of tennis balls and basketballs will not fit into the same container because the balls are different sizes. So why can the same number of differently sized gas molecules fit in the same container?

[The reason is that gases have an important property that is unlike solids and liquids.]

In a solid or liquid, the molecules are very close together. Gases are mostly made of empty space. Under normal conditions, the space taken up by gases is about 99.9 percent empty! There is a lot of space between the tiny molecules. And if there is a lot of space between gas molecules, then the size of the molecules has little effect on how many molecules fit in a given container.

Generally, Avogadro's law is only true for ideal gases, which do not exist in the real world. Real gases will not have exactly the same number of molecules at the same volume, temperature, and pressure. However, many real gases behave in a nearly ideal way so this law is pretty close.

KEY QUESTIONS

- What properties do the molecules in a liquid and gas have that allow that substance to move more than solids?

- Why is the concept of an ideal gas useful?

- How do the four gas laws work in relation to each other?

Ideas for Supplies ▼

- wooden dowel
- 3 small eyehooks
- 2 large plastic cups
- string
- masking tape
- 1000 mL graduated cylinder
- spring scales graduated in pounds or ounces
- several small household objects— erasers, dry beans, pencils, marbles, etc.

MEASURING MASS

Although they are related, mass and weight are not the same. Mass is the amount of matter in an object, while weight is a measure of the force of gravity on an object. An object's mass remains the same no matter where it is, and an object's weight varies depending on the force of gravity. For example, an object has the same mass on the earth as it does on the moon. Its weight, though, is very different because the gravitational pull on the earth is different from the gravitational pull on the moon. On the earth, an object's weight is very close to its mass and we often use the terms interchangeably.

In the metric system, the kilogram (kg) is the basic unit of mass. In this activity, you will build your own basic double pan balance and measure the mass of some common household items.

- **Attach an eyehook to the center of the wooden dowel, facing upward.** Attach the two remaining eyehooks to either end of the dowel, facing downward. Using a hole puncher, punch two holes on opposite sides of a plastic cup. Repeat with the second cup.

- **Thread a length of string through the holes on one cup and suspend it from one of the end eyehooks.** Repeat with the second cup and suspend it from the other end of the dowel.

- **Thread a string through the center eyehook.** Tie the string around a rod or other object so that the balance hangs freely.

- **Before you measure anything, you will need to check to see if the balance is evenly balanced.** Are the two cups hanging at the exact same level? If not, add small pieces of tape to the higher cup until the two cups are even.

- **To test the accuracy of your balance, use a spring scale to find an object's known mass.** Then measure the object using your balance. Place the object in one cup. Then slowly add water to the second cup until it is even and balanced. Pour the water into a graduated cylinder and note the volume. Because the density of water is 1 gram/milliliter, you can easily calculate the mass. The volume in milliliters is the same as its mass in grams. Compare the measured mass you found with the known mass of the object. Was there a difference?

- **Using your balance, measure the mass of several household objects.** Repeat your measurements. Is your balance accurate? Is it precise? Explain your findings.

THERE! IT'S READY TO GET TO WORK!

Inquire & Investigate

VOCAB LAB

Write down what you think each word means:

solid, crystal lattice, intermolecular forces, volume, compress, molecules, surface tension, liquid, gas, dense, kinetic molecular theory, pressure, ideal gas, and **significant figures**.

Discuss your definitions with friends using real-life examples. Did you all come up with the same definitions? Turn to the text and the glossary if you need help.

To investigate more, use your results to determine if your measurements have been affected by systematic or random error. Explain why or why not.

Ideas for Supplies ▼

- 25 pre-1982 pennies and 25 post-1982 pennies
- 50 mL or 100 mL graduated cylinder
- scale

USING DENSITY TO IDENTIFY UNKNOWN METALS

The content of U.S. coins has changed greatly through time. In earlier years, some coins were made with gold and silver, but those metals became too expensive. Pennies were made of copper until 1982, when the price of copper also became too expensive. Since 1982, pennies have been made with a thin layer of copper on the surface and another metal on the inside. In this activity, you will use density tests to determine what metal is inside different pennies.

- **Fill a graduated cylinder one-third full of water and measure the volume of water.** Keep a record of all of your measurements. Use a scale to determine the mass of the cylinder and water.

- **Add 20 or more of the pre-1982 pennies to the cylinder.** Measure the mass and volume of the cylinder and water with the pennies.

- **Calculate the density of the pre-1982 pennies by dividing the mass by the volume.** Repeat with the post-1982 pennies.

- **Review the following table of densities of various metals.** Compare them to your measurements. What metal do you think is inside the post-1982 pennies? Why?

DENSITY - G/ML	METAL
2.7	Aluminum
5.7	Tin
7.1	Zinc
7.9	Iron
8.9	Copper
8.9	Nickel
10.5	Silver
11.3	Lead
19.3	Gold
21.5	Platinum

To investigate more, remember that no experiment is perfect. Are there any systemic or random errors in your calculations? What might be a source of error in this experiment and how could it have affected your results?

DENSITY

Density is a measurement that compares the amount of matter in an object to its volume. Objects with a lot of matter in a specific amount of volume are denser. Objects with less matter in the same volume are less dense. The mass of the atoms in an object, their size, and how they are arranged determine its density. If the mass and volume of a substance are known, density can be calculated using this formula: density = mass ÷ volume.

Ideas for Supplies

- safety goggles
- paperclips
- clean wine corks
- beakers or cups
- substances to test, such as table salt, baking soda, boric acid, cream of tartar
- flame

FLAME COLOR GUIDE

Lithium (Li): red

Sodium (Na): strong, persistent orange

Potassium (K): pink-lilac

Rubidium (Rb): red-violet

Cesium (Cs): blue-violet

Calcium (Ca): orange-red

Strontium (Sr): red

Barium (Ba): pale green

Copper (Cu): blue-green, often with white flashes

Lead (Pb): greyish-white

IDENTIFY METAL IONS WITH A FLAME TEST

Chemists use a flame test to identify certain metal ions in a substance. When heated, the electrons in some metals gain energy and jump to higher levels. When they fall back, they release energy in the form of different colored light, depending on the kind of metal. In this activity, you will use a flame test to determine the presence of metal ions in a substance.

CAUTION: Use safety goggles and ask an adult to supervise.

- **Straighten a paperclip and stick one end into the wine cork.** In each beaker, mix one household ingredient with water to create a solution for testing.

- **Wearing safety goggles, light the flame.** Hold the cork and heat the wire end of the paperclip until it glows. Dip the hot end of the wire into the first solution. Take it out of the solution and hold it in the flame. Record your observations.

- **Repeat for each substance.** Use a new wire for each test. Did your flame test detect the presence of metal ions? Which metals did the flame test detect? In which substances were they detected?

To investigate more, test other household substances from your pantry for the presence of metal ions. Make a mixture of two substances and repeat the flame test. What color do you see? How do you explain this observation?

Chapter 3
Changing States of Matter

HOW DOES SOLID IRON BECOME...*LIQUID* IRON? IS THERE SUCH A THING?

How does matter change its state and go from being a solid to a liquid to a gas and back?

Matter changes its state when the molecules either gain or lose energy, which causes the force of attraction between them to weaken or strengthen.

What happens to an ice cube in hot weather? What happens to a puddle of water in the road on a sunny afternoon after a thunderstorm? Under certain conditions, solids, liquids, and gases can change forms. A solid ice cube can melt into a puddle of liquid water. A puddle of water can evaporate into water vapor, which is a gas.

As we learned in the previous chapter, the atoms and molecules of matter are always in motion, even if we can't see it. These moving parts have mass, even though they are tiny, and therefore have energy.

A moving object's energy is called its kinetic energy. If the object's speed increases, its kinetic energy also increases. When atoms and molecules are moving fast, they have more kinetic energy than when they are moving slowly.

What is temperature? Why is ice cream cold while soup is hot? When you measure temperature, you are measuring the average kinetic energy of that substance's atoms and molecules.

There are billions of moving atoms and molecules in a substance. Some move quicker and some slower. When they move and bump into each other, they transfer small amounts of energy. A substance with a higher average kinetic energy will have a higher temperature. A substance with a lower average kinetic energy will have a lower temperature.

MELTING: SOLID TO LIQUID

In a solid substance, atoms and molecules are strongly attracted to each other and locked in place, giving the solid its shape and volume. But the molecules are still moving and wiggling.

When a solid is heated, the molecules increase their motion. Eventually, their motion creates enough kinetic energy to overcome the attractions holding the molecules in place. The molecules are able to move more freely. Then, the solid substance changes state and becomes a liquid in a process called melting.

The temperature at which a solid substance melts into a liquid is called its melting point. Different substances have different melting points, depending on the strength of the attractions between its atoms and molecules. A substance with stronger attractions will need more energy in order for its atoms and molecules to overcome the attractions. For example, salt and sugar have two different melting points.

- Sugar's melting point is about 320 degrees Fahrenheit (160 degrees Celsius).

- Salt's melting point is much higher at 1,474 degrees Fahrenheit (801 degrees Celsius). This is because the attractions between the molecules in salt are much stronger than those in sugar.

CHEMISTRY CONNECTION

Pressure can change a substance's melting point. When pressure increases around a substance, the melting point also increases, making it easier to keep the substance a solid.

EVAPORATION: LIQUID TO GAS

Have you every left a cup of water on the table for several days? You might notice that the amount of water slowly decreases. What is happening? Where does the water go? The water is changing from a liquid into a gas, a process called evaporation.

In any liquid, molecules are constantly moving and bumping into each other. The molecules aren't locked in place, but attractions between these molecules hold them close to each other. When a molecule in a liquid has enough energy to overcome the forces holding it with other molecules, it escapes into the air as a gas.

> Different liquids evaporate at different rates because the attraction between different types of molecules can be weak or strong.

A liquid whose molecules are strongly attracted to each other will evaporate more slowly than a liquid whose molecules are held together by a weaker attraction. The liquid with a stronger attraction between its molecules needs more energy for its molecules to escape and change into a gas. Evaporation happens at the surface of a liquid, so liquids with more surface area experience more evaporation.

As the temperature of a liquid increases, the molecules move more and increase their kinetic energy. More molecules are able to escape into the air as a gas. When a liquid reaches its boiling point, the molecules spread out and form bubbles.

VAPOR PRESSURE

Molecules that evaporate from a liquid exert a pressure, called the vapor pressure of the liquid. As a liquid's temperature increases, the vapor pressure caused by evaporation of its molecules also increases. Eventually, when the vapor pressure of a liquid equals the vapor pressure of the surrounding gas, the liquid begins to boil. A liquid's boiling point is the temperature at which its vapor pressure equals 1 atmosphere (atm). Vapor pressure and boiling points differ for different liquids and depend on the strength of the bonds between the liquid's molecules. A liquid with a lower vapor pressure will have a higher boiling point than a liquid with a higher vapor pressure.

CONDENSATION: GAS TO LIQUID

Have you ever seen droplets of water on the outside of a cold glass? This happens when water vapor in the air changes from a gas into a liquid in a process called condensation.

When water vapor molecules in the air touch the cold glass, they transfer some of their energy to the glass and slow down. The molecules no longer have enough energy to overcome the attractions between them. They move together and form liquid water droplets on the glass. The faster the molecules join together, the faster the rate of condensation.

Temperature affects the rate of condensation. Cooler temperatures reduce the energy in the molecules of a gas, slowing their motion. When the motion becomes slow enough, the attractions among the molecules pull them together to form a liquid.

FREEZING: LIQUID TO SOLID

Freezing is the process of a liquid changing into a solid. It's the opposite of melting. When a liquid is cooled, its molecules lose energy and slow down. If it is cooled enough, the molecules slow down so much that their attractions pull them even closer together and fix them into place to form crystals. The liquid turns into a solid.

The temperature at which a liquid turns into a solid is called its freezing point. Different liquids have different freezing points, because of the differences in their molecules and attractions.

Instead of moving closer together when they lock into place to form a solid, water molecules actually move farther apart when they form solid ice crystals. In most solids, molecules are closer together in the solid.

ACCURACY VS. PRECISION

For chemists, accuracy and precision have very different meanings. Accurate data is close to its actual value. How tall are you? Five feet is an accurate measurement if you are actually five feet. Precision refers to how often a value can be replicated by the measuring instrument. If you weigh a book three times on the same scale and get 15.6 grams each time, the scale is precise, even if the book actually weighs 17.1 grams. If you weigh the book on a second scale and get 15.6, 16.2, and 17.3 grams, it is not precise. Data that is precise may not always be accurate. Data that is accurate, however, is always precise.

Watch a few dry ice experiments!

Steve Spangler dry ice

KEY QUESTIONS

- **What does matter need to change its phase? Why?**

- **Frost is an example of deposition and dry ice is an example of sublimation. Can you think of other examples of these phase changes?**

OTHER CHANGING MATTER

Some substances can change directly from a solid to a gas, skipping the liquid state entirely. Have you ever seen dry ice? Dry ice is frozen carbon dioxide (CO_2). At room temperature and normal pressure, the frozen CO_2 molecules move so fast that they break apart and become a gas rather than a liquid. This change, from a solid to a gas, is called sublimation.

What about going the other way? Under the right conditions, some gases can change directly into a solid, skipping the liquid phase entirely. This process, called deposition, is the opposite of sublimation.

Have you ever woken up on a cold morning to find the car's windshield covered in frost? Frost is an example of deposition. When there is the right amount of water vapor in the air and the temperature of the ground surface is low enough, the water vapor in the air changes directly into solid frost without becoming liquid water first.

EXPLORE EVAPORATION AND CONDENSATION

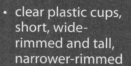
When water is heated, some liquid evaporates into the air as water vapor. As water vapor cools, it condenses and becomes liquid water. In this activity, you will explore the processes of evaporation and condensation with water.

CAUTION: Have an adult help with heating the water.

* **Heat about 1 cup of water until it is approximately 120 degrees Fahrenheit (50 degrees Celsius).** Pour the hot water into a short clear plastic cup until it is about two-thirds full.

* **Place the taller cup upside down inside the rim of the cup with water.** Wait a few minutes and observe what happens inside the cups.

* **Examine the sides and top of the tall cup with a magnifying glass.** Remove the top cup and feel the inside. Record your observations.

* **Explain what is happening inside the cups.** How does this activity demonstrate evaporation and condensation? What is happening to the water molecules?

> To investigate more, design another experiment that demonstrates evaporation and condensation. Share your experiment with your classmates.

Ideas for Supplies ▼

* clear plastic cups, short, wide-rimmed and tall, narrower-rimmed
* magnifying glass

VOCAB LAB

Write down what you think each word means:

kinetic energy, temperature, water vapor, melting point, sublimation, evaporation, vapor pressure, condensation, and **deposition.**

Discuss your definitions with friends using real-life examples. Did you all come up with the same definitions? Turn to the text and the glossary if you need help.

Ideas for Supplies ▼

- safety goggles and oven mitts
- distilled water
- graduated cylinder
- 3 medium flasks or small pots
- thermometer
- table salt
- sugar
- calcium chloride (ice melt)

THE BEST PASTA WATER HAS LOTS OF SALT. I WONDER WHY?

BOILING POINT OF WATER

Pure water boils at 212 degrees Fahrenheit (100 degrees Celsius). What happens if you add salt to the water? How will the dissolved salt, called a solute, affect water's boiling point? Adding solutes, such as salt, to water interferes with the water's ability to change from liquid to gas. The presence of the particles decreases the number of water molecules at the surface of the liquid. This lowers the vapor pressure and raises the water's boiling point. The water must be heated to a higher temperature in order for it to evaporate. In this activity, you will test how different solutes affect the boiling point of water.

CAUTION: Ask an adult to help you with boiling liquids and always wear safety goggles.

- **Heat approximately 50 milliliters of water in a flask.** Measure the temperature of the water when it begins to boil. Take several readings and average them to find the boiling point. Record your observations.

- **Repeat using 50 milliliters of water mixed with about 15 grams of sugar.** Repeat for each substance to be tested. Record your observations.

- **What happens to the water's boiling point when each solute is added?** How do you explain your results?

> To investigate more, see if changing the amount of solute affects the boiling point of water. Repeat the experiment using different amounts of the same solute. Does this have an effect on the water's boiling point? Why?

Chapter 4
Compounds, Mixtures, and Solutions

Why do we have many different kinds of matter if all matter is made of atoms?

There are many kinds of atoms and these atoms and molecules combine in different ways to form different kinds of matter.

All matter is made from atoms. Some substances, such as gold and copper, are elements. These are pure substances that are made from entirely one type of atom. Other types of matter are made from several different combinations of atoms. These substances can be compounds, mixtures, or solutions. It can be difficult to see the difference between a compound, mixture, or solution just by looking at it. You need to go deeper and understand how atoms combine in matter to identify each one.

ATOMS BOND TOGETHER

You've already learned that atoms are the building blocks for all matter. But what does this mean?

Imagine a stack of bricks. If you want to build a wall, you start by attaching one brick to another. As you continue, you'll attach more and more bricks. Sometimes, the bricks are identical, but other times, they might be different colors or sizes.

The strength of your wall depends on how strongly each individual brick is attached to the bricks around it. In a similar way, groups of atoms bond together to form molecules, which then join together to form the matter that we see all around us. A molecule consists of two or more atoms that are connected by chemical bonds. Molecules can be formed from many different combinations of atoms. Water (H_2O) is a molecule made from two hydrogen (H) atoms and one oxygen (O) atom. Hydrogen gas (H_2) is also a molecule, with two hydrogen atoms bonded together.

Why do atoms bond in the first place? Because they want to be happy! And having a full energy level of electrons is what makes an atom happy. Some atoms have only a few electrons on their outer shells and it's easiest to lose those to become stable. Others have a few open spots and find it easier to gain electrons to become stable. Together, they can solve each other's problems.

Atoms form two main types of bonds—ionic and covalent bonds. In an ionic bond, one atom donates an electron to another atom, which forms the bond.

When we say an atom wants to be happy, we don't mean that atoms have emotions. We describe an atom as being happy when all of its energy levels are complete. Just as people are happy when they have enough to eat, atoms are happy and stable when they have the right number of electrons to fill up their energy levels!

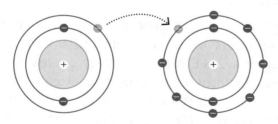

In a covalent bond, two atoms, each with an extra electron, share the two as a pair. By sharing, each atom fills its energy levels.

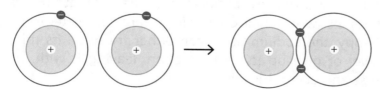

Using one of these types of bonds, two or more elements can chemically combine together to form a compound. A compound is a molecule made of two or more elements in specific ratios. It can be broken into simpler pieces—its individual elements. Compounds are homogeneous materials. This means that they are the same all the way through and have a uniform composition.

There are millions of different compounds. Distilled water is an example of a pure compound. Distilled water contains only water molecules (H_2O). Just as there are two different types of bonds, there are two different types of compounds—ionic and covalent.

IONIC COMPOUNDS

Sometimes, atoms gain or lose electrons, forming ions, or charged particles. The opposite charges of a negatively charged anion and a positively charged cation attract each other. When an anion sticks to a cation, it forms an ionic compound. One of the most common ionic compounds is sodium chloride (NaCl), also known as salt.

Let's look at this in a little more detail. Atoms with atomic numbers between 1 and 18 on the periodic table follow a 2-8-8 rule. Their first energy levels can hold two electrons. The second level can hold eight electrons and the third level is also full with eight electrons. Sodium (Na) is number 11 on the periodic table. This number tells us that a sodium atom has 11 protons and 11 electrons. Two electrons fill its first energy level. Eight electrons fill its second level. But that leaves one extra electron. Remember, atoms are happiest when their energy levels are complete. To be happy, the sodium atom can either try to fill its third level or give up its 11th electron, leaving it with full first and second levels.

At the same time, other atoms are looking to gain an electron or two. For example, chlorine (Cl) is element 17 on the periodic table. A chlorine atom has 17 protons and 17 electrons. Two electrons fill its first energy level. Eight electrons fill its second level. The third level is holding seven electrons.

> To be happy, chlorine needs one more electron to complete that third level.

Now we've got a chlorine atom that is searching for an extra electron and a sodium atom that has one to give. Together they can both be happy! Sodium can give its extra electron to chlorine and they both will have full energy levels.

When sodium gives up its extra electron, it becomes positively charged because now it has one proton more than electrons. When chlorine receives the extra electron, it becomes negatively charged. The two atoms with opposite charges are attracted to each other. This attraction forms the bond between them.

Electrolytes are compounds that conduct electricity when dissolved in water. Many ionic compounds are electrolytes.

Ions that have more than one atom are called polyatomic ions. Polyatomic ions are found in many ionic compounds. Some of the most common polyatomic ions are:

acetate ($C_2H_3O_2^{-1}$)

ammonium (NH_4^{+1})

bicarbonate (HCO_3^{-1})

carbonate (CO_3^{-2})

chromate (CrO_4^{-2})

cyanide (CN^{-1})

dichromate ($Cr_2O_7^{-1}$)

hydroxide (OH^{-1})

nitrate (NO_3^{-1})

nitrite (NO_2^{-1})

permanganate (MnO_4^{-1})

phosphate (PO_4^{-3})

sulfate (SO_4^{-2})

sulfite (SO_3^{-2})

Ionic compounds often have similar characteristics. These characteristics are the result of the strong attractions between the ionic compounds' anions and cations. Ionic compounds frequently form crystals when large groups of ions are stacked together in regular patterns.

Compared to other substances, ionic compounds also usually have high melting and boiling points. In order for an ionic compound to melt, there must be enough energy to pull the anions away from the cations and overcome the attraction between them. It takes a lot of heat to generate the amount of energy needed. This leads to high melting and boiling points.

Additionally, many ionic compounds are hard. Ions that stack together in a crystal are difficult to move and force apart. Even with a lot of force, the attractions between the anions and cations in the ionic compound hold it together, making it very hard. At the same time, an ionic compound can be brittle.

[The right force can separate the compound's cations and anions and cause the crystal to break apart and shatter.]

Another characteristic of ionic compounds is that they conduct electricity only when dissolved in water or melted. Normally, pure water is not a good conductor of electricity. However, when an ionic compound is added to the water, the water becomes a conductor. For example, when salts dissolve in water, they break into cation and anion particles. These moving ions carry electrical charge from one place to another, enabling the water to conduct electricity.

In solid form, the anions and cations of an ionic compound are locked in place, so it can't conduct electricity.

[When melted, the anions and cations are able to move and slide past each other to carry an electric charge.]

COVALENT COMPOUNDS

When two atoms get close to each other, the negatively charged electron from one atom feels a pull of attraction to a positively charged proton of another atom. This attraction pulls the two atoms close together, and the electrons of each atom feel attraction to the protons in both atoms. This type of bond is called a covalent bond. The electrons are attracted to and shared by both atoms, forming a covalent bond. In order for atoms to form a covalent bond, there needs to be space in the outer energy levels of both atoms. Atoms will covalently bond to each other until each atom's outer energy level is full.

Let's take a look at how this works with two chlorine (Cl) atoms. Each chlorine atom has 17 electrons. Two fill the first energy level, eight fill the second level, and there are seven in the third level. By sharing one electron, each chlorine atom can fill its third level. The two chlorine atoms stick together in a covalent bond and the shared pair of electrons is attracted to the nuclei of both atoms.

NAMING IONIC COMPOUNDS

Naming ionic compounds is pretty simple. First, find the two-word base name of the compound. The first word is the name of the cation. For example, for NaOH, the first word is sodium. The second word is the name of the anion. If it is a polyatomic ion, you can look at the list of polyatomic ions on page 52 for this word. In NaOH, the OH is hydroxide. Together, the compound's name is sodium hydroxide. If the anion is an element, then use the element's name ending in "ide." For example, in NaCl, the Na is sodium, while the Cl is chlorine. In the compound's name, the chlorine becomes "chloride." The name for NaCl is sodium chloride.

NAMING COVALENT COMPOUNDS

Like ionic compounds, covalent compounds have two-word names. The first word is the name of the first element in the compound's formula. The second word is the name of the other element, with the suffix "ide" placed at the end. For example, HBr is a covalent compound made from one hydrogen (H) atom and one bromine (Br) atom. It is called hydrogen bromide. Sometimes, a prefix is added to the names of the elements to show that there is more than one element present in the compound. For example, OCl_2 is called oxygen dichloride, adding the prefix "di" to represent the two chlorine atoms.

Two hydrogen (H) atoms can also be joined with a covalent bond. Each atom has one electron. By sharing their electrons, both atoms can fill their first energy level and be happy. When two hydrogen atoms bond together, the resulting hydrogen molecule is more stable than the individual hydrogen atoms. The covalent bond allows the electrons of each atom to be near two protons instead of just one. The pull of two protons in a hydrogen molecule (H2) is stronger and more stable than the pull of only one proton on a single hydrogen atom.

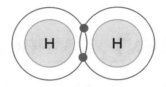

hydrogen molecule (H_2)

hydrogen atom

Covalent compounds share similar characteristics. The molecules in covalent compounds are not as strongly attracted to each other as the molecules in ionic compounds. As a result, covalent compounds usually have low melting and boiling points. Less energy is needed to separate molecules from each other because the forces holding them in place are weaker than those in ionic compounds.

Many covalent compounds are also poor conductors of electricity, which makes them good insulators. There are no mobile ions in a covalent compound to carry the electrical charge from one place to another. Also, many covalent compounds burn easily.

MIXTURES

Elements can also combine in mixtures. Most substances in nature are mixtures. Rocks, soil, food, and even air are all mixtures. Just about anything you can combine is a mixture. When you make a cake, the batter is a mixture of several different ingredients.

A mixture is different from a compound in several ways. First, the individual molecules do not chemically bond or change when they are mixed together. For example, salt water is a mixture—pure sodium chloride (NaCl) mixed with pure water (H_2O).

[
When water evaporates, the sodium chloride molecules remain behind and keep their same chemical properties.
]

A mixture can be homogenous, which means all of the molecules spread evenly throughout. Other mixtures are heterogeneous. The different molecules in the mixture are not spread uniformly throughout the substance, causing one part of the substance to have a higher concentration of one ingredient than another part.

Mixtures can be separated by physical forces. Grinding, boiling, distillation, filtering, and chromatography are all physical ways to separate mixtures and pull the distinct pieces apart. When you boil salt water, the water separates and evaporates into the air while the salt remains behind.

CHEMISTRY CONNECTION

Some molecules have both ionic and covalent bonds. In a sodium hydroxide (NaOH) molecule, the oxygen and hydrogen atoms are bonded together with a covalent bond to form the hydroxide molecule, while the sodium atom is bonded to the hydroxide molecule with an ionic bond.

Concrete is a mixture made from lime, cement, water, sand, and pieces of rocks and other solids. The concrete mixture hardens from a liquid into a solid. Inside the solid concrete, the pieces of rocks and gravel are not evenly spread throughout the slab. In addition, the rocks and gravel are not chemically bonded to the cement. Instead, physical forces hold them in place.

[Is concrete a homogenous or heterogeneous mixture?]

SOLUTIONS

Solutions are a type of mixture. In a solution, one material, called the solute, is completely dissolved in another substance, called a solvent. Groups of molecules are mixed and evenly distributed throughout the solution.

In this way, solutions are homogeneous systems. One example of a solution is sugar water. Solid sugar crystals dissolve and spread evenly throughout the water. There is the same amount of sugar in the water at the top or bottom of the glass.

A solution can also be a gas dissolved in liquid. Do you drink carbonated water? Sodas and seltzer are solutions in which molecules of carbon dioxide gas are dissolved in water.

Not all liquid mixtures are solutions. A suspension is an example of a mixture that is not a solution. For example, when a spoonful of flour is mixed with a cup of water, the flour's particles are not evenly spread out. They suspend in the water. Over time, the flour's molecules will settle on the bottom of the cup.

When you mix a solute and solvent, the solute begins to break into pieces. Stirring can make the dissolving process move faster. The solvent molecules rub against the solid surface of the solute molecules, removing them one by one. Eventually, the concentration of the two substances is even throughout the system.

[
Dilution is a process of adding solvent to a solution in order to reduce its concentration of solute.
]

Factors such as heat and pressure can affect how a solute dissolves. Heating a solvent allows it to dissolve more solids. That's why you might melt butter and sugar together over heat when making brownies or cookies. The heat helps the sugar dissolve.

A solution is a mixture of one substance, called a solute, that is completely dissolved in another substance, called a solvent. A solution's concentration is the amount of solute it contains.

CHEMISTRY CONNECTION

Hot water can dissolve more sugar than cold water, but it can dissolve less carbon dioxide gas.

POLAR WATER MOLECULES

Water molecules are made from two hydrogen (H) atoms and one oxygen (O) atom. Although the molecule shares electrons through covalent bonds, they are not shared equally. The oxygen atom more strongly attracts the electrons, pulling them more often to that end of the molecule. Because electrons have a negative charge, this makes the oxygen end of the water molecule have a bit of a negative charge. As a result, the hydrogen ends of the water molecule are slightly positively charged. When this happens, the molecule is called a polar molecule.

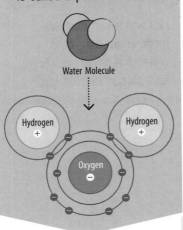

Water Molecule

Hydrogen ＋

Hydrogen ＋

Oxygen −

Increasing pressure allows a liquid to dissolve more gas. Have you ever opened a soda bottle? The pressure of the bottle keeps the carbon dioxide inside. But when you open the bottle, a rush of gas and bubbles release. If you open and close the bottle several times, it will release less gas and bubbles each time because the soda is no longer under such high pressure and less carbon dioxide remains dissolved in the soda solution.

[The amount of solute that can be dissolved by a solvent is called its solubility.]

Surface area affects solubility. Image a spoonful of sugar crystals or a solid sugar cube. Which do you think would dissolve more quickly in a glass of water? Those tiny sugar crystals overall have a larger surface area than the square sugar cube. More of the sugar molecules are exposed to the water at any point in time, which allows them to dissolve more quickly.

The solubility of a substance is measured by the number of grams that dissolve in 100 milliliters of water at a certain temperature. Because the amount of a substance that dissolves in water varies, each substance has different solubility.

Substances are made from different atoms and are bonded together differently, so it isn't surprising that they behave differently in water. Substances such as sugar have a higher solubility, which means that more grams dissolve in 100 milliliters of water. Sodium chloride has a lower solubility because fewer grams dissolve in 100 milliliters of water.

DISSOLVING

Dissolving happens when a solvent's molecules attract a solute's ions so much that it overcomes the attractions between the solute's ions. The solute's ions separate from each other and mix evenly throughout the solvent.

The polar characteristics of a molecule can affect how quickly it dissolves. Sodium chloride crystals, or salt, are made from positively charged sodium ions and negatively charged chloride ions.

A water molecule is a polar molecule, with positively and negatively charged ends. The positive end of a water molecule attracts the negative chloride ion. The negative side of a water molecule attracts the positive sodium ion. Because the attraction of the water molecules for the sodium and chloride ions are greater than the attractions holding the salt crystal together, the salt dissolves.

ELEMENT, COMPOUND, OR MIXTURE?

When facing an unknown substance, it can be difficult to know whether it is an element, a compound, or a mixture. Mixtures can be separated by several physical methods such as grinding, distilling, boiling, filtering, and chromatography. In this activity, you will attempt to separate the substance into components and analyze each in order to determine if the substance is an element, compound, or mixture.

- **Create a substance to test.** Combine the jelly beans, iron filings, sand, and table salt.

- **Examine the substance.** Do you think it is an element, mixture, or a compound? Is the matter chemically bonded? If you think it is a mixture, is it a homogeneous or heterogeneous mixture? Is it evenly mixed?

COMPONENT	HYPOTHESIS	FINDINGS
jelly beans		
iron filings		
sand		
table salt		

- **Create a chart in your science journal to record your hypothesis and track your findings.** You can use the table above as a model.

- **Create a plan to separate the jelly beans from the substance.** What method of separation will you use? Separate the jelly beans from the substance.

- **Examine the beans.** Is this component an element, mixture, or compound?

- **Repeat these steps for each component to separate them from the material.** What methods of separation did you use? Examine the iron, salt, and sand to determine if they are elements, compounds, or mixtures. Is the matter made of only one element or two or more elements from the periodic table? Record your methods and observations in your science journal.

To investigate more, use dry ingredients from your food pantry to create another substance. Analyze the matter and determine if it and its components are elements, compounds, or mixtures. What are some methods that you could use to separate your substance into its components?

Ideas for Supplies ▼

- jelly beans
- iron filings
- sand
- table salt
- bar magnet
- 100 milliliter beakers
- filter
- 40 milliliters water

CHEMISTRY CONNECTION

A colloid is a solution with bigger particles, which causes it to appear foggy or milky. Milk is an example of a colloid.

Ideas for Supplies ▼

- safety goggles
- coffee filters
- 4 different black markers (not permanent markers)
- isopropyl alcohol
- large cups
- masking tape
- pencils

SEPARATING MIXTURES WITH CHROMATOGRAPHY

Chromatography is one technique for separating mixtures. Paper chromatography is a physical method for separating a mixture into its individual components. The ink in a black marker may appear to be one substance, but a chromatography test may identify different components in the ink. In this activity, you'll investigate how chromatography can be used to separate an ink mixture into its individual component dyes or pigments, using filter paper as a separating medium and isopropyl alcohol as a solvent.

- **Put on the safety goggles.** It will be important in this experiment to keep track of which pen you are using on which coffee filter, so remember to label everything. Label each marker with a number.

- **Make four strips out of the coffee filters and label the top of each strip with a marker number.** Draw a thick horizontal line on each strip, about ¼ inch up from the bottom, using the appropriate marker.

- **Place a small amount of isopropyl alcohol in each of four large cups.** Tape the top of each filter strip to a pencil and dangle the strips so the bottom of the paper touches the alcohol, but the marker line remains dry.

- **Watch as the filter begins to absorb the alcohol and move up the filter.** Record your observations in your science journal. What happens when the alcohol meets the ink lines? Do the different color inks travel at different rates? The component dyes will react differently, depending on their solubility and ability to stick to the paper.

- **Take the paper out after five minutes and let it dry.** What happened to the black lines? Create a chart to record your observations. What colors did you observe for each marker? What differences and similarities did you see? Did the colors separate in the same order?

To investigate more, you can repeat this experiment using anything with dye, such as M&Ms, Skittles, or Reese's Pieces. You'll first need to let the candy's color dissolve in water by placing a piece of candy on a paper plate with a drop of water. Then you can dab the colored water onto a vertical filter strip and stand it in a cup with a half inch of isopropyl alcohol. Check the paper at several time intervals. What does it look like at 15 minutes? 30 minutes? An hour?

CHEMISTRY CONNECTION

An alloy is a mixture of two or more metals, or of a metal and another element. Examples of alloys include brass, which is an alloy of copper and zinc, and steel, which is an alloy of iron and carbon.

Chapter 5
Chemical Reactions

What happens during a chemical reaction?

A chemical reaction is when two substances combine to form a completely new substance.

Sometimes, when you combine two or more substances, something happens. If you mix carbon in the form of coal and oxygen with a little heat, they burn and become carbon dioxide. The substances change and become something entirely different. It's a chemical reaction!

WHAT IS A CHEMICAL REACTION?

A chemical reaction is the process by which one or more substances are transformed into one or more different substances. It's a little bit like cooking. What happens when you combine flour, eggs, sugar, and butter, and then add some heat? Your results—mouth-watering cookies—are very different from the parts you started with!

Chemical reactions happen all around you, every day. When you digest food in your stomach, a chemical reaction occurs. Burning candles causes a chemical reaction, as does burning gasoline to power a car.

A chemical reaction is different from a substance changing states or dissolving. Changing from a solid to a liquid or dissolving a substance in a solution is a physical change. No new substances are formed.

[
In a chemical reaction, a chemical change occurs and a new substance is created.
]

REACTANTS AND PRODUCTS

When you make a new recipe, you need to understand exactly what ingredients to use and what the outcome of the recipe will be. The same is true in chemistry. In a chemical reaction, the ingredients are called reactants. The new substance produced by the chemical reaction is called the product.

During a chemical reaction, the reactants interact with each other. The bonds between the atoms in the reactants are broken, which allows the reactants' atoms to rearrange themselves into new arrangements and form new bonds. This produces one or more products. It is important to know that although the atoms might rearrange during a chemical reaction, no atoms are gained or lost. The same number of atoms exists at both the beginning and the end of the chemical reaction.

SCIENTIFIC NOTATION

When working with very small or very large numbers, chemists use scientific notation. In this method, a number is written as a product of a number between 1 and 10 and a whole number power (called an exponent) of 10. The exponent tells how many times a number must be multiplied by itself.

For example:

$10^1 = 10$
$10^2 = 10 \times 10$
$10^3 = 10 \times 10 \times 10$

To write a number in scientific notation, move the number's decimal point to the left until it is a number between 1 and 10. The number of places that you move is the exponent:

$170 = 1.7 \times 10^2$

To write very small numbers, move the number's decimal point to the right until it is a number between 1 and 10. The exponent is negative:

$0.053 = 5.3 \times 10^{-2}$

I JUST DON'T KNOW WHEN CHEMICAL REACTIONS HAPPEN....

IS THERE A SURE SIGN?

I'D SAY THE SMOKE AND CHARRED REMAINS OF THAT KALE INDICATE A CHEMICAL REACTION PRODUCING A LOT OF CARBON.

Sometimes, a chemical reaction can create a product that is completely different from the original reactants. For example, hydrogen gas (H_2) is a very flammable gas. Oxygen gas (O_2) is not flammable by itself, but it enhances the burning rate of other substances. You might think that the combination of these two gases would produce a product that is extremely dangerous and flammable. But something entirely different emerges when hydrogen and oxygen combine in a chemical reaction.

$$\left[\text{The equation of a chemical reaction between hydrogen gas and oxygen gas is } 2H_2 + O_2 \rightarrow 2H_2O. \right]$$

Water! Instead of being flammable, water is used to put out fires!

SIGNS OF A CHEMICAL REACTION

When you combine substances, you do not always trigger a chemical reaction. For example, when you combine sugar and water, the sugar dissolves and forms a solution of sugar water. This is not a new substance. How do you know? How can you tell if a chemical reaction has occurred? There are a few observations that you can make to find out if a chemical reaction has occurred.

One clue that points to a chemical reaction is the presence of gas. When you mix liquid vinegar with solid baking soda, gas is produced. The gas is a new substance that indicates a reaction has occurred.

When two solutions are mixed and a solid forms, this suggests that a chemical reaction has occurred. The solid that is produced is called a precipitate. It does not dissolve in the solution. For example, when calcium chloride solution and sodium carbonate solution are combined, a precipitate called calcium carbonate forms.

If two substances are mixed and there is a color change, this might mean that a chemical reaction has occurred. The atoms in a molecule and the structure of the molecules determine how light interacts with a substance and gives the substance its color. If the color changes, this is evidence that the molecules in the substance have also changed in a chemical reaction.

A temperature change is another sign that a chemical reaction might have occurred. Some chemical reactions produce energy and create heat, while others use energy and absorb heat.

Energy is the capacity of something to do work or produce heat. Kinetic energy is caused by motion and how fast something moves. Potential energy is stored energy.

THE CHEMICAL EQUATION

Chemists use chemical equations to show what happens to the reactants and products in chemical reactions. To write a chemical equation, you need to know the chemical formulas of the reactants and the products. The states of the reactants and products can also be noted in the equation using the following:

- (g) gas
- (l) liquid
- (s) solid
- (aq) aqueous solution, or something that has been dissolved in water.

When balancing chemical equations, it is essential to understand what the coefficients represent. Coefficients represent the ratio of molecules to each other. Let's look at this equation:

$$N_2 + 3H_2 \rightarrow 2NH_3$$

The coefficient of 3 shows that the molecules of hydrogen and nitrogen react in a ratio of 3:1 with each other. It does not mean that there are only three hydrogen molecules in the reaction. Instead, the coefficients show that, for every three molecules of hydrogen, one molecule of nitrogen is needed—this is the ratio of hydrogen to nitrogen that is needed for the reaction to occur.

The reactants are written on the left side of the equation, while the products are written on the right side. This chemical equation tells us that a chemical reaction between hydrogen gas and oxygen gas forms water.

$$H_2\ (g) + O_2\ (g) \rightarrow H_2O\ (l)$$

reactants ⟶ ↑   ↑ ⟵ products

But something is still not quite right about this equation. Remember learning that no atoms are lost or gained during a chemical reaction? Let's take a look at our formula and count the atoms on both sides of the equation.

$$H_2 + O_2 \rightarrow H_2O$$

2 hydrogen, 2 oxygen ⟶ ↑   ↑ ⟵ 2 hydrogen, 1 oxygen

In the reactants, there are two atoms of hydrogen and two atoms of oxygen. In the product, there are also two atoms of hydrogen, but only one atom of oxygen. Where is the second oxygen atom?

In order to correctly write this chemical equation, we need to balance it and account for the second oxygen atom. Balancing a chemical equation is another way of saying that mass is conserved. This means that all of the atoms in the reactants are in the products, with no new atoms being created or destroyed during the chemical reaction.

To balance a chemical equation, we need to find a set of coefficients that results in both sides of the equation having the same number of atoms as each element. A coefficient in front of a molecule tells how many of a particular type of molecule there are.

To balance this equation, we'll need two oxygen atoms. By adding a coefficient of 2 in front of the water molecule, we can show there are two atoms of oxygen in the product.

$$H_2 + O_2 \rightarrow 2H_2O$$

2 hydrogen, 2 oxygen ———↑   ↑——— 4 hydrogen, 2 oxygen

But there are now four hydrogen atoms. To balance the hydrogen, simply add a coefficient of 2 in front of the reactant hydrogen molecule.

$$2H_2 + O_2 \rightarrow 2H_2O$$

4 hydrogen, 2 oxygen ———↑   ↑——— 4 hydrogen, 2 oxygen

If we count the atoms on both sides of the equation, we find there are four hydrogen atoms and four oxygen atoms before and four hydrogen atoms and four oxygen atoms after. The equation is balanced.

PRACTICE BALANCING CHEMICAL EQUATIONS

Try balancing the following equations.

1. $Mg + P_4 \rightarrow Mg_3P_2$

2. $CH_4 + O_2 \rightarrow CO_2 + H_2O$

3. $N_2 + H_2 \rightarrow NH_3$

4. $NaCl + F_2 \rightarrow NaF + Cl_2$

5. $CO_2 + H_2O \rightarrow C_6H_{12}O_6 + O_2$

6. $P + O_2 \rightarrow P_2O_5$

Check your answers in the resources in the back of this book.

The study of chemical reaction rates is called kinetics.

TYPES OF REACTIONS

When a chef prepares a meal, there are several different ways a dish can be cooked. Baking, broiling, grilling, and frying are all different cooking methods. Chemicals, too, react with each other in different ways. Chemical reactions can be grouped into main types.

Combustion reactions occur when molecules that have carbon and hydrogen, also called organic molecules, combine with oxygen. The reaction forms carbon dioxide, water vapor, and heat.

In synthesis reactions, small molecules combine to form larger ones. Decomposition reactions are the opposite of synthesis reactions. They break apart larger molecules to form smaller ones. In a single displacement reaction, a pure element switches places with another element in a compound. When two cations in two ionic compounds switch places, a double displacement reaction occurs. It's always helpful to know what you are going to get when you mix a bunch of ingredients. Knowing what type of reaction is going to take place can help chemists predict the reaction's products.

[This can be extremely useful to avoid creating a potentially explosive reaction!]

THE MOLE AND MOLAR MASS

Atoms and molecules are extremely tiny. It is virtually impossible to count them one by one. Instead, scientists have developed a way to count large numbers of atoms or molecules by using the mole. One mole of any substance is equal to 6.02×10^{23} molecules of that substance.

$$1 \text{ mole} = 6.02 \times 10^{23} \text{ particles}$$

This means that 1 mole of oxygen is equal to 6.02×10^{23} molecules of oxygen and 1 mole of carbon equals 6.02×10^{23} atoms of carbon.

Scientists use the mole to calculate molar mass, which is the weight of 1 mole of a chemical compound. In a chemical reaction, if you need 1 mole of carbon, it is impossible to count out 6.02×10^{23} molecules to use. But if a scientist knows how much 1 mole of carbon weighs, they can simply use a balance to measure out the amount needed. The molar mass of a substance is the weight of 6.02×10^{23} molecules of that material in grams. A molar mass unit is grams per mole (grams/mole). One mole of one substance will have a different weight than one mole of another substance, because some molecules are heavier than others.

STOICHIOMETRY

Understanding the relationship between reactants and products is the basis for an important part of chemistry, called stoichiometry (pronounced stoy-key-ah-meh-tree). Stoichiometry comes from two Greek words, *stoicheion*, which means "element," and *metron*, which means "measure." Stoichiometry is a way to use math to relate the quantities of reactants and products to each other in a chemical reaction.

Stoichiometry helps you figure out how much of each reactant is needed to produce a certain amount of product. One general approach can be used to solve many stoichiometry problems.

PERCENT YIELD CALCULATION

Sometimes, chemists make a mistake during a chemical reaction. When experimental errors happen, the reaction does not produce the exact amount predicted by the chemical equation. Do you want to know if you've done a good job with the reaction? Find out with a percent yield calculation.

Percent yield = (actual yield in reaction ÷ predicted yield from stoichiometry problem) × 100 percent.

Say you've mixed hydrogen and oxygen reactants and expect a reaction that will produce water. According to your stoichiometry calculations, you predict that the reaction will make 20 grams of water. But when you run the experiment, you only get 15 grams of water. In this case, the percent yield would be: (15 grams ÷ 20 grams) × 100 percent = 75 percent. While a 75 percent yield is pretty good, many chemists would prefer to see a percent yield over 90 percent in their reactions.

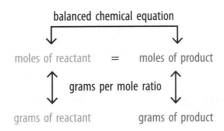

Using this chart, you can solve these problems easily. For example, if $N_2 + 3H_2 = 2NH_3$, how many moles of NH_3 can be produced from 8 moles of N_2?

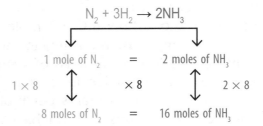

From the equation, we already know that 1 mole of N_2 reactant results in 2 moles of NH_3 product. Therefore 8 moles of N_2 would create eight times the moles of NH_3 ($8 \times 2 = 16$ moles of NH_3).

RATE OF CHEMICAL REACTIONS

Some chemical reactions take place very quickly. Others occur during a longer period of time. The rate of a chemical reaction measures how fast the reactants change into products. Several factors can affect the rate, including temperature, concentration of reactants, surface area of reactants, and the presence of a catalyst.

In order for a chemical reaction to occur, the reactant's molecules need to come in contact with other reactant molecules. As they bump into each other, they generate kinetic energy. With enough energy, the reactants can break apart and form new bonds to create the product. If the reactant's molecules do not have enough energy, they will not be able to break their bonds.

Sometimes, stoichiometry problems involve converting grams to moles and vice versa.

For example, how many grams of NH_3 are produced from 6.7 moles of N_2? Looking at the chart to the right, you know the moles of the reactant (N_2). The next step is to find moles of product (NH_3).

1 mole N_2 = 2 moles NH_3

$1N_2 \times 6.7 = 2NH_3 \times 6.7$

$6.7N_2 = 13.4NH_3$

Now we need to convert our answer of 13.4 moles of NH_3 into grams. NH_3 has a molar mass of 17.0 grams/mole.

$$13.4 \text{ moles } NH_3 \times \frac{17 \text{ grams}}{\text{mole}}$$

$13.4 NH_3 \times 17$ grams

$= 227.8$ grams NH_3

One way to affect the rate of a chemical reaction is to add heat. Heat increases the average kinetic energy of the reactants' molecules so that they move faster and bounce off each other with more energy. If this added energy causes more molecules to react, the rate of reaction increases.

The concentration of the reactants also influences the rate of reaction. When you walk through a crowded hallway, you bump into a lot more people than you would if the hall is deserted. When you increase the number of reactant molecules, they are more likely to bump against each other, which increases the likelihood of a chemical reaction.

Think about a big block of ice and a bunch of ice cubes. If both have the same mass, which will melt faster? The smaller ice cubes have more surface area and will melt faster. In a similar way, small reactants have more surface area on which a chemical reaction can take place.

Dissolving a reactant can also increase the rate of reaction. When a reactant dissolves, it separates into individual molecules or ions. This greatly increases the reactant's surface area.

Adding a catalyst can also increase the rate of a chemical reaction. A catalyst is a substance that speeds up a chemical reaction but does not become a product of the reaction. Common catalysts include the enzymes in your body that speed up biochemical reactions, such as when you are digesting food. A catalyst works by pushing the reactants together in a way that uses less energy and speeds up the reaction.

[
Understanding the factors that speed up reactions helps scientists tweak reactions to make them happen faster.
]

Inhibitors are the opposite of catalysts. They slow or stop chemical reactions.

DO ALL REACTIONS HAPPEN THE SAME WAY?

NOT AT ALL.

MANY THINGS AFFECT THE RATE AND PROCESS OF THE CHEMICAL REACTION, SUCH AS HEAT AND SURFACE AREA.... I'M MISSING ANOTHER....

GREAT SCOTT! *CATALYSTS!* I CAN'T FORGET THOSE. THEY PLAY A VITAL ROLE IN MANY REACTIONS.

As you've learned, reactants combine and form new products in a chemical reaction. But the process does not always end there. Sometimes, the products go through a reverse chemical reaction. Eventually, they return to where they started and become the original molecules again. Then, the process begins again. As this happens, the concentration of the molecules moves back and forth.

At some point, the forward and reverse reactions occur at the same rate. Although the reaction looks like it is finished, some molecules are still turning into products and other molecules are reforming reactants, but the concentrations of the molecules are no longer changing. When this happens, the system is at equilibrium. Equilibrium occurs when the rates of the forward and reverse reactions are equal. This does not mean, however, that there are equal amounts of reactants and products present.

When you add too much salt to water, not all of the salt can dissolve. It might not look as though anything is happening in this solution, but particles of sodium chloride are constantly dissolving, while other particles of sodium chloride are forming as precipitates.

[
Equilibrium occurs when each time a particle of sodium chloride dissolves, another forms as a precipitate.
]

Equilibrium occurs at the same point in the reaction and happens on its own without the help of outside forces. Two substances in a mixture will react by themselves and eventually reach equilibrium. At equilibrium, a system appears to have no charge.

CHEMISTRY CONNECTION

A reaction that goes to completion is when the reactants continue to react with each other until one is completely consumed.

Reactions can be reversible. The reactants form products and the products reform reactants. When the reactants' and products' concentrations have stabilized, the reaction is said to be at equilibrium.

Although equilibrium happens on its own, there are some factors that can change when equilibrium occurs.

- Adding new molecules or substances to the reaction

- Changing the temperature of the system

- Changing the pressure of the system

- Changing the concentration of the reactants or products

- Changing the total volume of the system

In the late 1800s, French chemist Henri Le Chatelier developed a rule about systems in equilibrium. Le Chatelier's principle says that, if you change the conditions of an equilibrium process, the equilibrium will shift in a way to minimize the effects of what you did. This means that if anything happens to interfere with equilibrium, the system will try to undo the change and move back to the original state of equilibrium.

FORMING A PRECIPITATE

Sometimes, when two liquids combine, a solid substance forms. This solid is called a precipitate. The new solid substance is a clue that a chemical reaction has occurred. Put on your safety glasses and mix 15 grams of Epsom salt and 100 milliliters of distilled water into a solution. Add 20 milliliters of ammonia to your solution. What happens? Observe for five minutes. Does a reaction occur? What evidence do you have?

KEY QUESTIONS

- **Name some examples of chemical reactions that occur in your daily life. How do you know these are chemical reactions?**

- **Why is it useful for chemists to express their work using chemical equations?**

- **What can you use to increase or decrease the rate of chemical reaction?**

Another way of expressing Le Chatelier's principle is that whatever is done to a system at equilibrium, the system will try to do the opposite.

Inquire & Investigate

VOCAB LAB

Write down what you think each word means:

precipitate, chemical reaction, combustion, coefficients, percent yield calculation, catalyst, and **equilibrium.**

Discuss your definitions with friends using real-life examples. Did you all come up with the same definitions? Turn to the text and the glossary if you need help.

FOAMING CHEMICAL REACTIONS

A chemical reaction occurs when the atoms and molecules of the reactants come in contact with each other. In a chemical reaction, one or more substances transforms into one or more new substances. In this activity, you will explore what happens when hydrogen peroxide (H_2O_2) decomposes into water (H_2O) and oxygen (O_2). Normally, this reaction occurs too slowly to watch, but by adding a catalyst, we can increase the rate of reaction.

- **Put on the safety goggles and wear rubber gloves.** This activity can be messy, so make sure you do it in a sink, tub, or other washable surface.

- **Use a funnel to carefully pour ½ cup of hydrogen peroxide into the soda bottle, avoiding contact with your eyes and skin.** Add 8 drops of food coloring to the bottle. Add 1 tablespoon of liquid dish soap and gently swirl the bottle's contents to mix.

- **In a small cup, mix 3 tablespoons of warm water and 1 tablespoon of dry yeast together.** Stir for about 30 seconds to dissolve the yeast.

- **Using the funnel, pour the water and yeast mixture into the bottle.** Stand back and watch what happens! Did the activity produce a chemical reaction? What clues did you observe to support your answer? What are the reactants in this activity? What are the products?

- **Write the chemical equation for this reaction.** Was there a catalyst in this activity? What was it? Is the catalyst included in your chemical equation? Why or why not? Was this an exothermic or endothermic reaction? Explain why. Record your observations and conclusions in your science journal.

> **To investigate more, repeat the experiment and vary the amount of yeast used. How does this change the results? What else can you vary? Does temperature affect the rate of the chemical reaction?**

Ideas for Supplies

- safety goggles
- rubber gloves
- funnel
- hydrogen peroxide (3-percent solution)
- clean 16-ounce plastic soda bottle
- food coloring (liquid, with a dropper)
- liquid dish washing soap
- small cup
- dry yeast
- warm water

CALCULATING MOLAR MASS

Calculating molar mass is not hard if you know the element's atomic mass from the periodic table. For compounds with multiple atoms, molar mass is found by multiplying the number of atoms of each element in the compound by their atomic masses.

For example, hydrogen has an atomic mass of 1.01 grams. The molar mass of a molecule of H_2 is $2 \times 1.01g = 2.02$ g/mol.

Following the same method, you can find the molar mass of compound NH_3. The atomic mass of hydrogen is still 1.01g and nitrogen is 14.01g. The molar mass of NH_3 is $(14.01g \times 1) + (1.01g \times 3) = 17.04$ g/mol.

PERCENT COMPOSITION

A percent composition calculation tells a scientist how much of a particular element is present in a chemical compound. It can be calculated using the following equation:

Percent composition of an element = (mass of the element/molar mass of the compound) × 100 percent.

- Using what you've learned about the mole and molar mass, calculate the molar mass of the following compounds.

   1. Na_2SO_4
   2. H_2O
   3. $Fe(OH)_3$
   4. C_2H_5OH

- Apply what you've learned to solve the following problems:

   1. A chemical equation calls for 0.125 moles of NaOH. How much of the compound do you measure in grams? (Hint: You'll first need to calculate the molar mass of NaOH.)

   2. How many moles of methanol (CH_3OH) are in 73.5g of methanol? (Hint: What is the molar mass of CH_3OH?)

   3. How many moles are in 17 grams of $CaCO_3$?

Check your answers in the resources in the back of this book.

Chapter 6
Acids and Bases

NOTHING LIKE A GREAT MEAL TO SEE ACIDS AND BASES AT WORK!

What makes a solution an acid or a base?

Solutions can be acids or bases, depending on the balance between hydrogen ions and hydroxide ions.

Have you ever heard someone talking about the acid in orange juice or the pH of a fish tank? Do you wonder what they mean? Welcome to the chemistry world of acids and bases!

Lots of things around you are either acidic or basic. Many fruits, such as oranges and lemons, are acidic. Carbonated beverages and tea are two drinks that are acidic. Substances such as baking soda, ammonia, soap, and antacids are basic. Even plain water can be an acid or a base. What makes something an acid or a base?

SELF-IONIZATION OF WATER

The first step in understanding acids and bases is looking at the behavior of water molecules. A plain water molecule is pretty simple—it contains two hydrogen atoms bonded with an oxygen atom (H_2O). Sometimes, water molecules can react with each other and change.

When two water molecules bump into each other and react, a proton from one of the hydrogen atoms can transfer to the other water molecule. The electron from that atom is left behind. Because a hydrogen atom only has one proton and one electron, it is as if a positive hydrogen ion (H^+) transfers from one molecule to the other. The following chemical equation shows this reaction:

$$H_2O + H_2O \rightarrow H_3O^+ + OH^-$$

Because the H_3O^+ ion has one more proton than electron, it is positively charged. The opposite happens for the other water molecule. It is as if it has lost a hydrogen atom and so it becomes a hydroxide ion (OH^-). Because it has an extra electron, the hydroxide ion is negatively charged.

[
In pure water, the H_3O^+ and OH^- ions balance each other out, making it a neutral liquid.
]

EXPLAINING ACIDS AND BASES

The first theory explaining acids and bases was proposed by a Swedish scientist named Svante Arrhenius in the late 1800s. He believed that all acids contained hydrogen atoms (H), which became hydrogen ions (H^+) when mixed with water. He also believed that all bases released the hydroxide ion (OH^-) in water. Because pure water has an equal balance between H^+ and OH^- ions, Arrhenius believed that when an acid or base was mixed with the water, it upset the balance and created a solution that was either acidic or basic.

Although Arrhenius's theory explained some behaviors of acids and bases, it had limits. For example, the theory did not explain how ammonia (NH_3) acted as a base even though it did not have a hydroxide ion. Scientists Johannes Bronsted and Thomas Lowry came up with an explanation and suggested that acids and bases could be identified by their behavior in a reaction.

Under this theory, an acid in an aqueous solution acts as a proton (H^+) donor. It transfers a proton to a water molecule, which results in more H_3O^+ in the solution. The solution has a higher concentration of H_3O^+ than OH^-, making it acidic.

Bases act in an opposite manner. When a base is added to water, the base molecule takes a proton from a water molecule. This is why bases are called proton acceptors. When the base takes a proton from a water molecule, it leaves more hydroxide ions (OH^-) in the solution. The H_3O^+ molecules in the solution react with the OH^- molecules, take a proton back, and form H_2O again. This causes the concentration of H_3O^+ to decrease in the solution, making it basic.

Acids and bases often have specific chemical and physical properties. These properties can be used to tell the difference between an acid and a base.

PROPERTY	ACID	BASE
Taste	Sour	Bitter
Smell	Often burns nose	Often odorless
Texture	Sticky	Slippery
Reactivity	Reacts with metals to form H_2 molecules	Reacts with oils and fats
Electrical conductor	Yes	Yes

STRENGTH AND CONCENTRATION

Some acids can make holes in pieces of metal. Other acids, such as citric acid in orange juice, are safe to eat. What makes one acid strong and another acid weak?

The strength of an acid is determined by its ability to donate a proton, which increases the H_3O^+ in the solution. Strong acids almost completely disassociate, or break apart, in water. For example, almost every molecule in the acid HA breaks apart into H^+ and A^- ions when placed in water. All of the H^+ ions attach to water molecules, producing a lot of H_3O^+ in a solution. Saying an acid is strong means that it breaks apart into ions almost completely in water. The following are some common strong acids.

- HCl – hydrochloric acid

- HBr – hydrobromic acid

- HI – hydriodic acid

- HNO_3 – nitric acid

- $HClO_4$ – perchloric acid

- H_2SO_4 – sulfuric acid

These acids ionize 100 percent, or break apart completely, in water. For example, HCl breaks into H^+ and Cl^- ions. Because HCl is a neutral molecule, when the H^+ ion breaks off, the remaining Cl^- ion is negatively charged.

The molecules of a weak acid are much less likely to disassociate and break apart when placed in water. As a result, they produce a smaller amount of H_3O^+. The majority of acids are weak. One mole of weak acid may only provide $1/1000$ mole of H_3O^+.

ACID AND THE OCEANS

When carbon dioxide gas (CO_2) in the atmosphere increases, some goes into the ocean. There, the carbon dioxide reacts with water, making the ocean water more acidic by creating an acid called carbonic acid:

$$H_2O + CO_2 \rightarrow H_2CO_3$$

Carbonic acid affects the pH of the ocean waters. Normally, the ocean is slightly basic. Adding this extra acid makes the ocean less basic and more acidic. This change in pH can have a negative effect on sea life. Have you seen pictures of coral reefs that look bleached? These coral reefs suffer from ocean acidification.
You can see photographs here.

NOAA features climate coral reefs

ACIDS ARE A COMMON PART OF COOKING, USED IN ALMOST EVERYTHING FROM DRESSINGS TO DESSERT.

I KNOW THAT MOST OF THE YUMMY STUFF WE LOVE CONTAINS ACIDS, SUCH AS FRUIT, SAUCES, AND SODA. WHAT SORT OF FOODS USE BASES?

ANYTHING WITH A BITTER TASTE USUALLY HAS BASES INVOLVED...SUCH AS THIS TRADITIONAL DISH FROM NORWAY: LUTEFISK! THEY USE LYE, A BASE, TO COOK IT.

Like acids, some bases are strong, while others are weak. A strong base completely disassociates in water, while a weak base only partially disassociates. In a base, the ion that breaks off is hydroxide (OH^-). The following are several common strong bases.

- LiOH – Lithium hydroxide (Li^+ and OH^-)
- NaOH – Sodium hydroxide (Na^+ and OH^-)
- KOH – Potassium hydroxide (K^+ and OH^-)
- RbOH – Rubidium hydroxide (Rb^+ and OH^-)
- CsOH – Cesium hydroxide (Cs^+ and OH^-)
- $Ba(OH)_2$ – Barium hydroxide (Ba_2^+ and $2OH^-$)

The concentration of an acid or base is the amount of acid or base in a solution. Concentration is different from strength. A strong acid or base can have a low concentration if there is not very much of it in a solution. A weak acid or base can have a high concentration if there is a large amount of it in a solution.

pH SCALE

Scientists use the pH scale to measure if a liquid is acidic or basic. The pH scale measures the concentration of hydrogen ions (H^+) and hydroxide ions (OH^-).

The scale has values from 0 to 14. Pure water, which is neutral, measures 7 on the pH scale. A liquid with a higher concentration of H_3O^+ ions than OH^- ions is an acid. Acids measure between 0 and 7 on the pH scale. If a liquid has a lower concentration of H_3O^+ ions than OH^- ions, it is a base. Bases measure between 7 and 14 on the pH scale.

Most liquids that you might use have a pH near 7. Some chemicals can be very acidic or basic. Battery acid is a very strong acid with a pH less than 1. Drain cleaner is a base with a pH near 14.

One of the ways to determine if a solution is acidic or basic is to use indicators. Indicators are substances that turn one color in an acidic solution and another color in a basic solution. One common indicator is litmus, which turns red in an acid and blue in a base.

ACIDS AND BASES IN EVERYDAY LIFE

Acids and bases are an important part of daily life. Your stomach uses acids to digest the food you eat. From medicines to cleaning products, companies use acids and bases to make products that people use every day. For example, sulfuric acid is used to make fertilizers, fibers, paint, and dyes. Sodium hydroxide, a base, is used in making fabrics, paper, and cleaning products.

Acids and bases are also common in products at home. The sour taste in many foods is caused by the acids in them. For example, the sour-tasting vinegar that makes salad dressings and pickled vegetables taste so good is actually diluted acetic acid.

[
Some sour-tasting foods that include acids are oranges, lemons, and wine.
]

Because of their unpleasant, bitter taste, bases are not typically used in foods. Yet bases can be found in many other everyday items. The caffeine in coffee and nicotine in cigarettes are both alkaloids, which is a class of base than contains nitrogen. The bitter taste of tonic water comes from quinine, another alkaloid base. Antacid medicine, which works to neutralize excess stomach acids, often contains bases. Several cleaners contain bases. Lye is a strong base used in oven cleaners, drain cleaners, and hair-removal lotions.

Toothpaste contains sodium fluoride, a weak base that helps to kill bacteria in your mouth when you brush your teeth.

CHEMISTRY CONNECTION

A buffer is a solution that resists changes in pH when small quantities of an acid or a base are added to it. A buffer is a mixture of a weak acid and the base that is formed when that acid donates a proton when mixed with water.

ACID RAIN AND THE ENVIRONMENT

TITRATION

Because acids and bases neutralize each other, they can be used to determine the concentration of a known acid or base in a solution. This procedure, called a titration, slowly adds a solution of a known concentration to a solution of unknown concentration until the solution becomes neutral. At the neutral point, the moles of acid in the solution are equal to the moles of base added to make the solution neutral.

KEY QUESTIONS

- What does a substance need to release to become an acid? What does it need to release to become a base?
- What are some of the properties of acids and bases?
- What can a pH scale tell you about a substance?

All living things need water to live. Rain is an important part of the water cycle. In some cases, though, the rain carries acid from pollution. This causes harm to the environment and living creatures. Acid rain occurs when power plants, factories, cars, and homes burn fossil fuels, which release acidic gases into the air. These gases mix with clouds. When the clouds release rain, snow, sleet, or fog, acid rain falls to the ground.

Acid rain affects everything it touches. Acids remove minerals from the leaves of trees, from plants, and from the soil. Without these minerals, the trees and plants cannot grow properly. Weakened plants and trees are more susceptible to disease and weather conditions.

[
Lakes and aquatic ecosystems can be greatly damaged by acid rain that either falls directly on the water or enters through rivers and streams.
]

As the lake becomes more acidic, some fish and aquatic species die. In Scandinavia, thousands of lakes have been ravaged by acid rain, leaving no surviving species.

Acid rain also damages buildings and homes. The acid eats into the structure's metal and stone and damages stained glass and plastics. Buildings made from more reactive materials, such as marble, are more vulnerable to acid rain and more easily damaged. Many ancient buildings have been damaged by acid rain, including the Parthenon in Greece and the Taj Mahal in India.

ACID OR BASE?

Scientists use litmus paper as one way to test if a solution is acidic or basic. Red litmus paper turns blue when in the presence of a base, while blue litmus paper remains unchanged. In the presence of an acid, the blue paper turns red, while the red paper does not change. In this activity, you will test several household substances and determine if they are an acid, a base, or neutral. Don't forget to wear safety goggles.

- **Pour a small amount of each substance to be tested into its own clear plastic cup.** Dip a small piece of red litmus paper into the first substance. Record your observations in your science journal. Then dip a small piece of the blue litmus paper into the first substance. Record those observations. Is the substance an acid or a base?

- **Test each substance with red and blue litmus papers.** Keep track of your conclusions. Which substances are acidic? Which are basic? Are any of the substances that you tested neutral? Explain your results.

> To investigate more, mix a solution of 50 percent water and 50 percent carbonated soda. Repeat the litmus testing. Does diluting the soda change your results? Test different concentrations of soda. What theory can you propose about the sensitivity of the litmus paper test? Repeat this testing with other substances. Do your observations fit with your theory?

Ideas for Supplies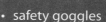

- safety goggles
- carbonated soda
- tap water
- distilled water
- toothpaste
- shampoo
- soap
- vinegar
- lemon juice
- red and blue litmus paper

VOCAB LAB

Write down what you think each word means:

acid, base, aqueous, pH scale, titration, and **litmus**.

Compare your definitions with those of your friends or classmates. Did you all come up with the same meanings? Turn to the text and glossary if you need help.

Chapter 7

The Nucleus and Radioactivity

TRUST ME, THERE ARE SOME MIGHTY POWERFUL FORCES IN THE HEART OF AN ATOM!

What happens during a nuclear reaction?

An atom's nucleus can be transformed through a nuclear reaction, which can cause the atom to change from one element to another.

In a chemical reaction, the bonds between atoms are broken and reformed. There are changes in how each atom's electrons are shared with or donated to other atoms. The atom's nucleus, however, does not change in a chemical reaction.

A nuclear reaction is what is needed to affect the nucleus of an atom. In a nuclear reaction, the particles in an atom's nucleus—the protons and neutrons—are changed. When this happens, an atom of one element can transform into an atom of another element. Nuclear chemistry is a branch of chemistry that studies nuclear reactions and how the reactions change the nuclei of certain atoms.

RADIOACTIVE DECAY

Atoms like to be stable. They are most stable when their outer energy levels are filled with electrons, which they accomplish by either gaining or losing electrons or sharing them with other atoms. None of this changes the atom's nucleus or the particles within it.

Sometimes an atom will have an unstable nucleus. An unstable nucleus can spontaneously undergo changes to its protons and neutrons in a process called radioactive decay. During this process, the atom's nucleus becomes more stable. At the same time, energy and/or particles are released from the nucleus. An isotope that undergoes a spontaneous breakdown of its nucleus, releasing some form of radiation, is called a radioisotope.

When radioactive decay changes the nucleus of an atom, the number of protons and/or neutrons in the atom can change. If only the number of neutrons changes, the atom changes into another isotope of the same element. However, when the number of protons changes, the atom transforms into another element altogether.

Some isotopes are naturally radioactive. Atoms of elements with atomic numbers greater than 83, which means they have more than 83 protons, are naturally radioactive. This means that if they're left alone, they will undergo nuclear reactions until they are eventually transformed into isotopes of elements with atomic numbers less than 83.

THREE TYPES OF NUCLEAR DECAY

There are three major types of nuclear decay that radioisotopes can undergo.

- alpha decay
- beta decay
- gamma radiation

During each type, the nucleus of a radioisotope emits a particle to become more stable. These products are called nuclear emissions.

CHEMISTRY CONNECTION

Isotopes are atoms of the same element that have a different number of neutrons. As a result, isotopes of the same element have different atomic masses.

Nuclear reactions produce a great deal of energy. They result in much larger energy changes than chemical reactions.

Chemists have a special way of writing an isotope in chemical and nuclear equations. When writing two types of carbon isotopes, the top number is the mass number, the number of protons and neutrons in the isotope. The bottom left number is the isotope's atomic number, or just the number of protons:

Carbon-14: $^{14}_{6}C$

Carbon-12: $^{12}_{6}C$

In this example, each carbon isotope has the same number of protons (6) but different numbers of neutrons:
14 - 6 = 8 and 12 - 6 = 6.

In alpha decay, the atom's nucleus emits an alpha particle, which is made of two protons and two neutrons, or a helium nuclei. The loss of two protons in alpha decay transforms the original atom into an element with an atomic number that's two lower. For example, when an atom of uranium (U) emits an alpha particle, it decays into the element thorium (Th). Its atomic mass also changes, decreasing by 4. The following equation shows this nuclear reaction.

$$^{238}_{92}U \rightarrow \, ^{4}_{2}He + \, ^{234}_{90}Th$$

mass number
(# of protons + # of neutrons)

$$^{238}_{92}U \rightarrow \, ^{4}_{2}He + \, ^{234}_{90}Th$$

atomic number
(# of protons)

The alpha particle has a +2 charge and is very large and heavy. It is also relatively slow moving. As a result, alpha particles can be blocked easily by air, paper, clothing, and skin. Even so, alpha particles can be dangerous to living organisms if they are inhaled or swallowed because they can damage the linings of the lungs and other internal organs. For example, the element radon emits alpha particles when it decays. This is why it is important to have a radon detector in your house.

[
When inhaled, alpha particles can cause damage to humans and have been linked to lung cancer.
]

Beta decay occurs when a neutron turns into a proton and an electron is emitted from the atom. This happens when an atom's nucleus has too many neutrons.

For example, one isotope of hydrogen has one proton and two neutrons. This hydrogen isotope is very unstable. When it undergoes beta decay, one of its neutrons transforms into a proton and releases an electron. This turns the isotope into a helium isotope with two protons and one neutron. It increases the isotope's atomic number by one, but has very little change on the atomic mass.

$$^3_1H \rightarrow ^0_{-1}e + ^3_2He$$

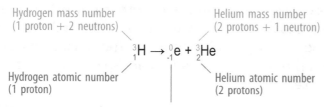

Hydrogen mass number
(1 proton + 2 neutrons)

Helium mass number
(2 protons + 1 neutron)

$$^3_1H \rightarrow ^0_{-1}e + ^3_2He$$

Hydrogen atomic number
(1 proton)

Helium atomic number
(2 protons)

releases a negative-charged electron

Beta particles have a - charge and are high energy and very light. They are a lot smaller than alpha particles and can penetrate deeper into living matter. Because of this, beta particles can cause some damage to living cells or cause genetic change to a cell's nucleus. A sheet of aluminum can shield against beta particles.

Gamma decay occurs when an atom's nucleus has too much energy. To stabilize it, the nucleus releases very high-energy light called gamma rays. Because no changes in the atom's protons and neutrons occur, the atom's atomic number and mass remain the same. High-energy gamma rays can be very harmful to living organisms. A thick layer of lead is needed to block this type of radiation.

[Gamma rays can be used to sterilize medical equipment and to treat certain types of cancer.]

CHEMISTRY CONNECTION

Nuclear transmutation happens when a nucleus undergoes decay and transforms into a different element.

BINDING ENERGY AND MASS DEFECT

If you add up the mass of all the protons and neutrons in an atom's nucleus, their sum is a number that is slightly larger than the actual mass of the nucleus. What happened to the rest of the mass? This missing mass is called the mass defect. It has been converted into binding energy that is released to hold the nucleus together.

FISSION VS. FUSION

There are two main types of nuclear reactions—fission and fusion. In a nuclear fission reaction, the heavy nucleus of a large atom is split into two or more pieces. When this happens, the nucleus releases neutrons and energy.

Nuclear fission can happen spontaneously. Other times, it occurs when an atom's nucleus is hit by a particle. The hit causes the neutrons of the nucleus to be emitted. As these released neutrons hit other nuclei, they can cause a chain reaction, with more nuclei splitting and emitting energy and neutrons. The chain reaction continues until all of the nuclei are split and the atoms are stable.

When the nucleus breaks apart, it releases some binding energy that was holding it together. In nuclear fission, the combined mass of the smaller nuclei that are formed is smaller than the original atom's mass. According to Albert Einstein's formula, energy = mass × speed of light^2 ($E = mc^2$), scientists know that mass and energy are directly related. When one decreases, the other increases. Therefore, in a nuclear fission reaction, as mass decreases it is released in the form of energy. As a result, nuclear fission produces a lot of heat.

NUCLEAR POWER PLANTS

Nuclear fission is used to create power in nuclear power plants. Nuclear power plants split atoms, usually uranium atoms, to produce heat energy. They use this energy to heat water, which is converted to steam to power a turbine generator that creates electricity. Nuclear fission also provides energy for nuclear-powered ships and submarines.

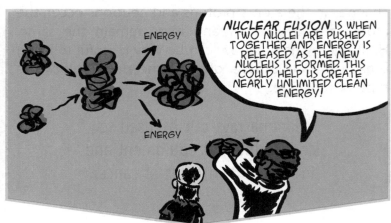

Nuclear fusion is the opposite of fission. In nuclear fusion, energy is released when two small atoms combine to form a larger and more stable atom. This releases even more energy than nuclear fission. The sun produces energy from nuclear fusion by fusing hydrogen atoms together to form helium. Currently, there is no known way to harness fusion energy in a power plant. Scientists hope to harness the energy of nuclear fusion one day.

HALF-LIFE

The half-life of a chemical reaction is the time it takes for half of the reactants to be converted into products. In a nuclear reaction, the half-life is the amount of time it takes for half of the radioisotopes to decay.

Radioactive materials decay at very different rates. Some decay very quickly, while others decay during billions of years. Every isotope has its own half-life. Isotopes with a longer half-life are more stable and will take longer to decay.

Carbon is an essential element for living organisms. Carbon-14 is a radioactive isotope of carbon with a half-life of about 5,730 years. Every 5,730 years, half of the carbon-14 isotopes in a dead organism decay into nitrogen. By measuring the amount of carbon-14 remaining in a fossil, scientists can estimate the age of the fossil.

KEY QUESTIONS

- How is a nuclear reaction different from a chemical reaction?
- What needs to happen in the atom's nucleus for the atom to change into a different element?
- What is the difference between nuclear fission and nuclear fusion?

NUCLEAR MEDICINE

Nuclear medicine uses small amounts of radioactive material to diagnose or treat several diseases, including cancer, heart disease, and gastrointestinal disorders. Patients swallow, inhale, or receive an injection of a radioactive material called a radiotracer. The radiotracer travels through the body and accumulates in the organ or body area to be examined. A special camera or imaging machine detects radioactive emissions from the radiotracer. This information helps doctors identify disease at early stages.

Doctors also use nuclear medicine to treat certain diseases and disorders. For example, doctors use small amounts of radioactive material to treat cancer. Targeting cancer cells with radiation can kill the cancer cells and stop them from dividing.

Ideas for Supplies ▼

- small objects such as candies, coins, or beads to use as protons and neutrons
- periodic table (page 117)
- ribbons or other material to model energy release

CHEMISTRY CONNECTION

Nuclear plants typically use uranium for nuclear fission. Uranium is a common metal found in rocks around the world. Atoms of uranium-235 are easily split apart.

CREATING A FISSION MODEL

In nuclear fission, the atom's nucleus changes and splits apart, at the same time generating large amounts of energy. Only a small number of atoms undergo fission under normal circumstances. Nuclear power plants use uranium-235 atoms to produce energy.

At the power plant, scientists fire neutrons at the uranium-235 atoms. When a neutron hits an atom's nucleus, it is absorbed and the atom becomes uranium-236. Now unstable, the uranium-236 atom wants to split apart. It breaks into two smaller nuclei, krypton-92 and barium-141.

In the process, the uranium-236 atom releases three neutrons and a tremendous amount of energy. Fission continues as the emitted neutrons hit other uranium-235 atoms and split those nuclei. In this activity, you will create a fission model, using an atom of uranium-235.

- **First, create a model of a uranium-235 nucleus.** Consult a periodic table to determine the correct number of protons and neutrons in the atom's nucleus. Is this atom considered large or small?

- **Using another neutron, simulate it hitting and being absorbed by the uranium-235 nucleus.** What happens to the nucleus? What new atoms are formed? Change your model to reflect what happened. Use the periodic table to determine the correct number of protons and neutrons in each atom's nucleus.

- **After modeling the two smaller nuclei, do you have any neutrons left over?** What happens to them?

- **Model the energy released from the fission reaction.** Where does this energy come from?

> **To investigate more,** consider that when a nuclear fission chain reaction gets bigger and bigger, it can become an uncontrolled chain reaction. If it's allowed to continue and if there is enough uranium-235 present, the energy produced from the reaction can cause a big explosion. Use your model to demonstrate how a chain reaction occurs in nuclear fission.

VOCAB LAB

Write down what you think each word means:

nuclear chemistry, radioactive decay, radioisotope, alpha decay, beta decay, gamma decay, fission, fusion, and **half-life.**

Discuss your definitions with friends using real-life examples. Did you all come up with the same definitions? Turn to the text and the glossary if you need help.

Chapter 8
Other Branches of Chemistry

WOAH...CHEMISTRY SEEMS LIKE SUCH AN IMPORTANT FIELD TO STUDY! I WONDER WHAT OTHER SCIENCES USE IT?

What others areas of science involve the study of chemistry?

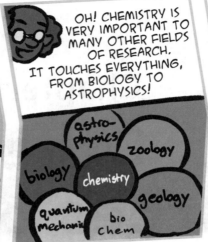

Chemistry is part of many different fields, including electrochemistry, organic chemistry, and biochemistry.

Chemistry is an integral part of learning about the world around us. It is known as the "central" science, because its concepts are at the core of several other branches of science. Chemistry touches physics, biology, geology, and more. Within chemistry, some chemists focus on specific areas of study, including electrochemistry, organic chemistry, and biochemistry.

ELECTROCHEMISTRY

Have you ever used a battery to power a flashlight or a radio? If so, you have used electrochemistry. Electrochemistry is a field of chemistry that uses the energy in chemical reactions to produce electric currents. In a flashlight, a chemical reaction in the batteries changes chemical energy into electrical energy, which is then turned into light.

One of electrochemistry's core concepts is the idea of an ion's oxidation state. An uncombined element is neutral and has an oxidation state of 0.

When an element gains or loses an electron in a chemical reaction, its oxidation state is no longer neutral. Its oxidation state becomes the number of electrons it has gained or lost compared to its neutral state. If an atom loses an electron in a chemical reaction, its oxidation state increases. The atom has been oxidized. If an atom gains an electron in a chemical reaction, its oxidation state decreases. It is reduced.

For example, when an atom of sodium reacts with an atom of chlorine, the sodium atom gives up one electron. Its oxidation state becomes +1. When the chlorine atom accepts the electron, its oxidation state becomes -1. The positive or negative sign of an atom's oxidation state matches the value of the ion's electrical charge.

In electrochemistry, an oxidation-reduction reaction, called a redox reaction, occurs when both oxidation and reduction reactions occur. A redox reaction changes the oxidation state of one or more elements.

[
Redox reactions are the
basis of ionic bonds.
]

The exchange of electrons in a redox reaction can be used to create an electric current in an electrochemical cell. An electrochemical cell has two metal electrodes separated by an electrolyte solution. The electrode where oxidation occurs is the anode. The electrode where reduction occurs is the cathode.

In one example, the anode is made of zinc, while the cathode is made of copper. When the ions in the electrolyte come in contact with the electrodes, redox reactions take place. At the zinc anode, a chemical reaction between the zinc metal and the electrolyte solution causes the zinc atoms to lose electrons and form zinc ions.

During an oxidation reaction, electrons are lost, while during a reduction reaction, electrons are gained.

CHEMISTRY CONNECTION

An atom that accepts an electron is called an oxidizing agent, while an atom that loses an electron is called a reducing agent.

The released electrons travel along a conducting wire to the reduction cell because they are attracted to the positively charged ions near the cathode. At the cathode, copper ions in the electrolyte solution accept the electrons that have traveled from the anode and become copper atoms.

A battery is an example of an electrochemical cell. Turning on a battery-powered flashlight completes an electrical circuit. The electrons released at the battery's anode flow through the circuit toward the cathode, carrying electrical current. They pass through the flashlight's bulb and light it. The electric current re-enters the battery at the cathode end.

CHEMISTRY CONNECTION

Electrochemistry can be used to remove impurities from a metal. Impure copper can be purified by electrolysis so that it can be used as a conductor. In an electrochemical cell, the copper ions in impure copper at the anode are attracted and travel through a solution to the cathode, where they are deposited as pure copper atoms. Any impurities in the copper are left behind at the anode and form a sludge.

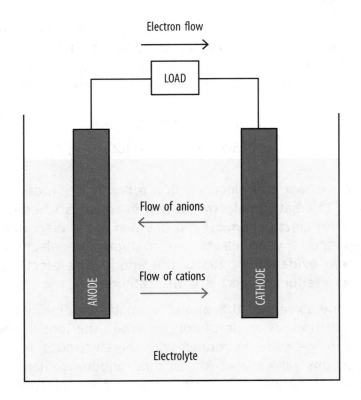

ORGANIC CHEMISTRY

One of the largest branches of chemistry, organic chemistry is the study of compounds that contain the element carbon (C). These are known as organic compounds. Carbon is an essential element for all living organisms. It is in our bodies, in the food we eat, and in the fragrances we smell. Carbon is more than a simple element. It can form in a wide variety of structures and combinations to create a seemingly endless number of compounds. Organic compounds are in many of the objects we use every day, from plastics and paint to antibiotics and soap. Organic chemists study the properties, structure, and chemical reactions of organic compounds.

[
By learning about organic compounds, chemists can understand more about living things and how they work.
]

Among the atoms, carbon atoms are unique because they like to bond to each other. Many organic compounds have a long chain or ring-shaped structure. In different molecules, the rings and chains might be different sizes and can be attached to atoms of other elements. Other elements that are commonly found in organic compounds include hydrogen (H), oxygen (O), nitrogen (N), phosphorus (P), and sulfur (S). Some organic molecules are small, while others are large. Some have single bonds, while others have double or even triple bonds.

Carbon atoms have four valence electrons, which they share with other atoms in a covalent bond.

JUST ADD HYDROGEN!

Not all substances that contain carbon are organic compounds. For example, a diamond is made from carbon atoms but is not considered organic. Carbon monoxide (CO) and carbon dioxide (CO_2), are also not considered organic compounds, even though they are made with the carbon element. Most organic compounds also have a carbon-hydrogen bond.

Organic compounds have several common characteristics. They are held together with covalent bonds. Many organic compounds are very sensitive to heat. Have you ever burned a piece of toast? You learned firsthand that organic compounds can burn easily at relatively low temperatures! Organic compounds also tend not to be as soluble in water as inorganic salts. However, when placed in an organic solvent, such as ether or alcohol, organic compounds are more soluble than salts.

Although there are millions of organic compounds, scientists have divided them into categories based on the non-carbon elements in the compound. Because they have similar molecules, compounds in the same category have similar properties. One category, the hydrocarbons, are formed from only hydrogen and carbon atoms. These two elements can form many different compounds.

One of the simplest hydrocarbons is methane (CH_4), which is a colorless, odorless gas. Methane is quite flammable. In a molecule of methane, one carbon atom links to four hydrogen atoms by common electron pairs. The molecule forms in the shape of a tetrahedron with the carbon atom in the middle.

Hydroxyls are another category of organic compounds. These organic molecules contain an oxygen atom bonded to a hydrogen atom. Hydroxyls belong to a group called alcohols. The majority of alcohols are colorless liquids at room temperature. Common alcohols include methanol and ethanol.

Although organic compounds are found in all living organisms, they can also be created by chemists in labs. This process is called organic synthesis. Chemists have created millions of organic compounds that have helped people around the world. Many objects used every day are made by organic synthesis in large factories. Plastics, alcohols, rubber, and dyes are manufactured with factory-made organic compounds.

[
Man-made organic compounds are also used to create synthetic dyes instead of using plants for dyes.
]

Inorganic compounds are all compounds that are not based in carbon-hydrogen bonds.

BIOCHEMISTRY

Are you interested in living organisms? Biochemistry is the study of chemistry in living things. From photosynthesis in plants to digestion in your stomach, biochemistry is involved in every chemical process and change that occurs inside you and in every other living thing on the planet. Metabolism, medicine, cellular biology, genetics, and nutrition are all areas of biochemistry.

Biochemists focus on organic molecules and the chemical processes and reactions that occur within living organisms. Organic biological molecules include amino acids, proteins, carbohydrates, fats, lipids, and nucleic acids. Amino acids are the building blocks for proteins.

CHEMISTRY CONNECTION

Carbohydrates are another type of biological compound found in living organisms that need them to survive. Some common carbohydrates are glucose and fructose.

Enzymes are proteins that function as catalysts to speed up chemical reactions in an organism. Fats, lipids, and carbohydrates are built from organic compounds and are essential for proper functioning in the body. Even an organism's instruction manual, its DNA, is made from organic molecules called nucleic acids.

Biochemistry looks at how an organism's cells communicate with each other and how the structure of a molecule can be related to its function within the body. Using this information, biochemists can predict how molecules will interact with each other. They can also explain why organisms survive, how food breaks down, and why disease occurs. Biochemists learning about the characteristics of keratin in hair can improve shampoos. Others might create safer food additives or develop artificial sweeteners. Some biochemists are working to develop targeted medicines that affect cells in specific ways.

> Biochemistry can be applied in genetic research, medicine, biotechnology, pharmaceuticals, and many other industries.

KEY QUESTIONS

- Why do so many fields of science incorporate the study of chemistry?
- Why is it important to have a basic understanding of chemistry?

BUILD A HOMEMADE BATTERY

Using the principles of electrochemistry, you can create your own battery at home. A copper penny and a galvanized nail will be your electrodes, while lemon juice will act as the electrolyte solution.

- **Carefully make a small cut on one side of the fruit.** Insert a penny in the cut on the lemon.

- **Push a nail into the other side of the lemon, making sure that it does not touch the penny.** Wrap one end of the wire around the nail, then connect it in the middle to the LED bulb.

- **Take the open end of the wire and touch it to the penny.** What happens? Why? Record your conclusions in your science journal. Create a diagram to explain how chemical energy was converted into electrical energy and used to light the LED bulb.

> **To investigate more, consider ways to make the lemon battery stronger. Create a new experimental design to increase the voltage of the battery.**

THIS WILL BE SOME FRESH-SMELLING ENERGY!

Inquire & Investigate

Ideas for Supplies ▼

- lemon
- small knife and cutting board
- copper pennies
- galvanized nails (coated with zinc)
- metal wire
- LED bulb

VOCAB LAB

Write down what you think each word means:

electrochemistry, organic chemistry, biochemistry, redox reaction, anode, cathode, and **organic synthesis**.

Discuss your definitions with friends using real-life examples. Did you all come up with the same definitions? Turn to the text and the glossary if you need help.

GLOSSARY

acid rain: rain that is polluted by acid in the atmosphere and damages the environment.

acid: any material that can accept a pair of electrons and has a pH less than 7.

agriculture: growing plants and raising animals for food and other products.

alcohol: any organic compound in which a hydroxyl group (–OH) is bound to a saturated carbon atom.

alkaline: having a pH greater than 7.

allotropes: different structural forms of an element in which the atoms of the element are bonded together in a different way.

alloy: a mixture of two or more metals, or of a metal and another element.

alpha decay: when a nucleus breaks apart and emits a helium nucleus, called an alpha particle.

amu: a unit of measurement, atomic mass unit, used to measure the mass of atoms and molecules.

anion: an atom or group of atoms with a negative charge.

anode: the electrode where oxidation occurs.

aqueous solution: a solution in which the solvent is water.

atmosphere: a unit of measure of pressure.

atom: the smallest particle of matter that cannot be broken down by chemical means. An atom is made up of a nucleus of protons and neutrons, surrounded by a cloud of electrons.

atomic mass: the sum of the number of protons and neutrons in an atom's nucleus.

atomic number: the number of protons in an atom's nucleus.

atomic symbol: the symbol that represents an element on the periodic table.

Avogadro's law: a law that states that the molar volumes of all ideal gases are the same.

base: a substance that accepts a hydrogen ion (H+) from another substance. Examples include baking soda, ammonia, and oven cleaner.

basic: having a pH lower than 7.

beta decay: a kind of radioactive decay of an atomic nucleus when an electron called a beta particle is emitted.

biochemistry: the study of chemistry in living things.

biology: the study of life and of living organisms.

boiling point: the temperature at which a liquid boils.

Boyle's law: a gas law that states that the pressure and volume of a gas have an inverse relationship, when temperature is held constant.

carbon: an element found in all organic compounds.

catalyst: a material that increases the rate of a chemical reaction without being consumed in the reaction.

cathode: the electrode where reduction takes place.

cation: an atom or group of atoms with a positive charge.

cellular biology: the study of cell structure and function.

characteristic: a feature of a person, place, or thing, such as blue eyes or curly hair.

Charles's law: a gas law that describes how gases expand when heated, and the relationship between volume and temperature.

chemical equation: the use of symbols to represent a chemical reaction, with reactants on the left and products on the right.

chemical reaction: a process where one or more substances are chemically charged and transformed into different substances.

chemistry: the study of the properties of substances and how they react with one another.

chromatography: a method of separating a mixture by passing it through a third material.

coefficients: the numbers placed before the reactants and products in a chemical equation so that the number of atoms in the products on the right side of the equation are equal to the number of atoms in the reactants on the left side.

combustion: a chemical reaction that produces heat and light.

composition: the ingredients in a mixture or substance.

compound: a pure substance made of two or more elements in specific proportions.

compress: to press or squeeze something so that it fits into a smaller space.

concentration: the volume of an ingredient divided by the total volume of a mixture.

condensation: the process in which a gas becomes a liquid.

conductivity: the ability to allow electricity to flow through a substance.

conversion factor: a number used to multiply or divide a quantity when converting from one system of units to another.

covalent bond: a type of bond that involves sharing a pair of electrons between atoms.

covalent compound: a compound that is created when two or more atoms are held together using covalent bonds.

crystal lattice: the structure in which ions or atoms are stacked in regular patterns to form a crystal.

data: information often given in the form of numbers.

decomposition: a chemical reaction where larger molecules break into smaller molecules.

density: the amount of matter in a give space, or mass divided by volume.

deposition: the process in which a gas directly becomes a solid, without becoming a liquid first.

dilution: the process of adding solvent to a solution to reduce its concentration of solute.

dissolve: to break up or be absorbed by a solvent.

distillation: the process of heating a mixture of materials to separate them.

electrical charge: a property of matter. Protons have a positive charge and electrons have a negative charge.

electrochemistry: the study of electricity and how it relates to chemical reactions.

electrode: the place where oxidation or deduction occurs in a voltaic cell.

electrolyte: a compound that, when dissolved in water, causes water to conduct electricity.

electron configuration: a list of orbitals that hold an atom's electrons.

electron: a negatively charged particle that is found in orbitals outside the nucleus of an atom.

element: a substance that cannot be broken down into simpler substances.

endothermic: a reaction that needs energy to take place.

enzymes: catalysts in biochemical reactions.

equilibrium: the point at which the products and the reactants of a chemical reaction have stabilized and the rates of forward and backward reactions are the same.

evaporation: the process in which a liquid becomes a gas.

exothermic: a reaction that generates energy in the form of heat.

experimental error: the difference between a measurement and the true value.

extract: to remove or take out by effort or force.

factor label method: a way to convert units from one type to another using a conversion factor.

ferment: to go through a chemical change that results in the creation of alcohol.

flame test: a test used to detect the presence of certain metal ions.

GLOSSARY

flammable: easily burned.

gamma radiation: the very high energy electromagnetic radiation that is released when a nucleus undergoes radioactive decay.

gas: one of the three states of matter. The particles of a gas are not bound to each other and move very fast in all directions. A gas does not have a definite shape or volume.

Gay-Lussac's law: a gas law that states that the density of an ideal gas at constant pressure varies inversely with the gas's temperature.

genetics: the study of how characteristics are passed from one generation to the next through genes.

geology: the scientific study of the history and physical nature of the earth.

graphite: a common black or gray mineral used as lead in pencils.

half-life: the amount of time it takes for half of a reactant to be converted to product in a chemical or nuclear process.

heterogeneous: something that is unevenly mixed.

homogenous: something that is completely mixed with a uniform composition.

ideal gas: a gas that follows all the rules of kinetic molecular theory.

indicator: a compound used to determine whether a solution is acidic or basic.

inhibitor: a material that decreases the rate of a chemical reaction.

intermolecular force: a force that holds covalent molecules to one another.

international system of units (SI): a system of units based on the metric system used by scientists.

ion: a particle with either a positive or negative charge.

ionic bond: a type of bond that transfers a valence electron from one atom to another.

ionic compound: a compound formed when a cation and anion combine with each other.

isotope: an atom of an element that has a different number of neutrons.

kinetics: the study of chemical reaction rates.

kinetic energy: energy caused by an object's motion.

Le Chatelier's principle: a rule that states when the conditions of equilibrium change, the equilibrium shifts to minimize the effects of the changes.

limiting reactant: the reactant that runs out first in a chemical reaction and determines the amount of products that can be formed.

liquid: one of the three states of matter. The particles of a liquid cluster together and flow. A liquid has a definite volume, but takes the shape of its container.

litmus: used with filter paper to test for acidity.

mass: the amount of material that an object contains.

matter: any material or substance that takes up space.

melting point: the temperature at which a solid changes into a liquid.

metabolism: chemical reactions within living cells that are necessary for life.

metalloid: an element with properties of both metals and nonmetals.

metric system: a system of weights and measures based on the number 10.

mineral: a substance found in nature that is not an animal or a plant.

mixture: a substance created by two or more substances that are combined physically but not chemically.

molar mass: the weight of one mole of a substance.

mole: a measurement of atoms and molecules. One mole of a substance equals 6.02×10^{23} molecules of that substance.

molecule: a group of atoms bonded together, the simplest structural unit of an element or compound. Molecules can break apart and form new ones, which is a chemical reaction.

nanoparticle: a microscopic particle where size is measured in nanometers.

neutron: a particle in the nucleus of an atom that does not have a charge.

nuclear emissions: particles released during a nuclear reaction.

nuclear fission: a nuclear reaction that releases energy when the nucleus of an atom splits into smaller pieces.

nuclear fusion: a nuclear reaction in which the nuclei of two or more atoms collide at a very high speed and join to form a new nucleus.

nucleus: the center of an atom, which holds protons and neutrons.

octet rule: the way that elements want to gain or lose electrons to have full outer energy levels of eight electrons.

orbit: the path an electron follows around an atom's nucleus.

orbitals: regions of space outside the atom's nucleus where electrons can be found.

ore: a naturally occurring mineral that contains metal.

organic compound: a type of compound that contains the element carbon and often hydrogen, as well as other elements.

organic: something that is or was living.

organism: a living thing.

oxidation: the loss of electrons or an increase in oxidation state by a molecule, atom, or ion.

oxidizing agent: a compound that causes another compound to be oxidized.

particle: an extremely small piece of something.

pascal: a unit of measurement of pressure.

percent yield calculation: a measurement of the accuracy of the result in a reaction, calculated by dividing the actual yield of a chemical reaction by the theoretical yield.

periodic table: a chart that shows the chemical elements arranged according to their properties.

pH: a scale used to tell the acidity of a solution, with the value of 7 being neutral.

physics: the study of physical forces, including matter, energy, and motion, and how these forces interact with each other.

polyatomic ion: an ion that has more than one atom.

potential energy: energy that is stored.

precipitate: a solid created from a chemical reaction in a solution.

pressure: a force that pushes on something.

product: the result of a chemical reaction.

property: a characteristic quality or distinctive feature of something.

proton: a positively charged particle in the nucleus of an atom.

radiation: small particles released during the radioactive decay of an atom's nucleus.

radioactive decay: when a nucleus spontaneously breaks apart and forms smaller particles.

radioactive: something that undergoes radioactive decay.

radioisotope: any radioactive isotope.

random error: a source of error in an experiment or chemical reaction that cannot be predicted or compensated for.

ratio: a comparison of two numbers or measurements, dividing one number by the other.

reactant: an ingredient in a chemical reaction.

redox reaction: a reaction in which the oxidation state of the reactants changes.

reducing agent: a compound that causes another to be reduced.

GLOSSARY

scientific notation: a method that scientists use to write very large or very small numbers.

significant figures: the number of digits in a measured or calculated value that give meaningful information.

simple displacement reaction: a reaction where an element replaces another element in a compound.

solid: one of the three states of matter. The particles of a solid are bound tightly. A solid has a definite shape and volume and does not flow.

solubility: the property of a substance to dissolve in a liquid called a solvent.

solute: the substance that is dissolved in a solution.

solution: a homogenous liquid mixture.

solvent: the substance that dissolves a solute.

sphere: a round object, such as a ball.

spontaneous: randomly.

stabilize: to hold steady.

states of matter: the form that matter takes. There are three common states of matter: solid, liquid, and gas.

stoichiometry: a way to relate the masses or volumes of reactants and products in a chemical reaction to each other.

sublimation: the process in which a solid becomes a gas without first becoming a liquid.

substance: the physical material from which something is made.

surface area: the total area of the surface of an object.

surface tension: the tendency of liquids to keep a low surface area.

suspension: a heterogeneous mixture that includes solid particles.

synthesis: the combination of smaller molecules to form larger ones.

theory: an unproven idea used to explain something.

titration: using a neutralization reaction to find out the concentration of an acid or base.

Torr: a unit of pressure.

valence electrons: the number of s and p electrons beyond the most recent noble gas.

volume: a measure of how much space an object occupies.

METRIC CONVERSIONS

Use this chart to find the metric equivalents to the English measurements in this activity. If you need to know a half measurement, divide by two. If you need to know twice the measurement, multiply by two. How do you find a quarter measurement? How do you find three times the measurement?

ENGLISH	METRIC
1 inch	2.5 centimeters
1 foot	30.5 centimeters
1 yard	0.9 meter
1 mile	1.6 kilometers
1 pound	0.5 kilogram
1 teaspoon	5 milliliters
1 tablespoon	15 milliliters
1 cup	237 milliliters

RESOURCES

BOOKS

Antoine Lavoisier: Genius of Modern Chemistry (Genius Scientists and Their Genius Ideas), Lisa Yount, Enslow, 2015.

Basher Science: Chemistry, Dan Green, Kingfisher Books, 2014.

Chemical Reactions (Science Readers: Content and Literacy), Jenna Winterberg, Teacher Created Materials, 2015.

The Complete Idiot's Guide to Chemistry, Ian Guch, Alpha Books, 2011.

Discoveries in Chemistry That Changed the World (Scientific Breakthroughs), Rose Johnson, Rosen, 2015.

Energy from Nuclear Fission: Splitting the Atom, Nancy Dickmann, Crabtree Publishing Company, 2015.

Molecules: The Elements and the Architecture of Everything, Theodore Gray, Black Dog & Leventhal Publishers, 2014.

Who Invented the Periodic Table? (Breakthroughs in Science and Technology), Nigel Saunders, Arcturus Publishing, 2010.

Why Is Milk White? & 200 Other Curious Chemistry Questions, Alexa Coelho, Chicago Review Press, 2013.

CHEMISTRY EXPERIMENTS

Chemistry Experiments (Facts on File Science Experiments), Pamela Walker and Elaine Wood, Facts on File, 2010.

Chemistry Experiments in Your Own Laboratory (Design, Build, Experiment), Robert Gardner, Enslow, 2015.

Cool Chemistry Activities for Girls (Girls Science Club), Jodi Wheeler-Toppen, Capstone Press, 2012.

Junk Drawer Chemistry: 50 Awesome Experiments That Don't Cost a Thing, Bobby Mercer, Chicago Review Press, 2015.

Super Cool Chemical Reaction Activities with Max Axiom, Agnieszka Biskup, Raintree, 2015.

The Totally Irresponsible Science Kit: 18 Daring Experiments for Young Scientists, Sean Connolly, Workman Publishing, 2015.

WEBSITES

Chemical Elements: Visit this site for an interactive periodic table. *www.chemicalelements.com*

Chemistry for Kids: This website has chemistry experiments, videos, projects, games, and fun facts. *www.sciencekids.co.nz/chemistry.html*

Middle School Chemistry: The website from the American Chemical Society offers lesson plans, experiments, and videos on topics such as matter, chemical reactions, density, and more. *www.middleschoolchemistry.com*

The pH Factor: Find interesting experiments students can do to learn more about acids and bases. *www.miamisci.org/ph*

Radar's Chem4Kids: Visit this website for basic information about a variety of chemistry and science topics. *www.chem4kids.com*

Radiation – RadTown USA: Learn more about radiation at this website from the Environmental Protection Agency. *www3.epa.gov/radtown*

RESOURCES

QR CODE GLOSSARY

Page 7: www.khanacademy.org/math/arithmetic/decimals/significant_figures_tutorial/v/significant-figures

Page 7: www.chem.sc.edu/faculty/morgan/resources/sigfigs

Page 9: www.wsdot.wa.gov/Reference/metrics/factors

Page 16: en.wikipedia.org/wiki/History_of_the_periodic_table#/media/File:Dmitry_Mendeleyev_Osnovy_Khimii_1869-1871_first_periodic_table.jpg

Page 16: www.pbslearningmedia.org/resource/phy03.sci.phys.matter.ptable/periodic-table-of-the-elements

Page 16: www.periodicvideos.com/index.htm

Page 44: www.youtube.com/watch?v=KG-qWeZm-LA

Page 85: www.noaa.gov/features/climate/coralreefwatch.html

Page 106: archive.org/details/agj0158.0001.001.umich.edu

EQUATION ANSWERS

Page 10

1. 2,678,400 seconds
2. 76.9 kilograms
3. 443.3 meters
4. 92 cookies
5. The painter will need 16 gallons of paint. The paint will cost him $272.

Page 22

1. Oxygen
2. 24.305
3. 13 electrons
4. Ag
5. Metalloids = 7, non metals = 17 (includes noble gases and hydrogen)
6. 26
7. 20 protons, 20 neutrons, 20 electrons
8. 24
9. Zinc
10. 11 protons, 12 neutrons, 11 electrons

Page 71

1. $6Mg + P_4 = 2Mg_3P_2$
2. $CH_4 + 2O_2 = CO_2 + 2H_2O$
3. $N_2 + 3H_2 \rightarrow 2NH_3$
4. $2NaCl + F_2 \rightarrow 2NaF + Cl_2$
5. $6CO_2 + 6H_2O \rightarrow C6H_{12}O_6 + 6O_6$
6. $4P + 5O_2 \rightarrow 2P_2O_5$

Page 80

1. 142.04 g/mol
2. 18.015 g/mol
3. 106.866 g/mol
4. 46.068 g/mol
1. 4.999 grams
2. 2.294 moles
3. 0.1698 moles

PERIODIC TABLE

1 H hydrogen 1.0079																	2 He helium 4.0026
3 Li lithium 6.941	4 Be beryllium 9.0122											5 B boron 10.811	6 C carbon 12.011	7 N nitrogen 14.007	8 O oxygen 15.999	9 F fluorine 18.998	10 Ne neon 20.180
11 Na sodium 22.990	12 Mg magnesium 24.305											13 Al aluminium 26.982	14 Si silicon 28.086	15 P phosphorus 30.974	16 S sulfur 32.065	17 Cl chlorine 35.453	18 Ar argon 39.948
19 K potassium 39.098	20 Ca calcium 40.078	21 Sc scandium 44.956	22 Ti titanium 47.867	23 V vanadium 50.942	24 Cr chromium 51.996	25 Mn manganese 54.938	26 Fe iron 55.845	27 Co cobalt 58.933	28 Ni nickel 58.693	29 Cu copper 63.546	30 Zn zinc 65.38	31 Ga gallium 69.723	32 Ge germanium 72.64	33 As arsenic 74.922	34 Se selenium 78.96	35 Br bromine 79.904	36 Kr krypton 83.798
37 Rb rubidium 85.468	38 Sr strontium 87.62	39 Y yttrium 88.906	40 Zr zirconium 91.224	41 Nb niobium 92.906	42 Mo molybdenum 95.96	43 Tc technetium [98]	44 Ru ruthenium 101.07	45 Rh rhodium 102.91	46 Pd palladium 106.42	47 Ag silver 107.87	48 Cd cadmium 112.41	49 In indium 114.82	50 Sn tin 118.71	51 Sb antimony 121.76	52 Te tellurium 127.60	53 I iodine 126.90	54 Xe xenon 131.29
55 Cs caesium 132.91	56 Ba barium 137.33	57–71	72 Hf hafnium 178.49	73 Ta tantalum 180.95	74 W tungsten 183.84	75 Re rhenium 186.21	76 Os osmium 190.23	77 Ir iridium 192.22	78 Pt platinum 195.08	79 Au gold 196.97	80 Hg mercury 200.59	81 Tl thallium 204.38	82 Pb lead 207.2	83 Bi bismuth 208.98	84 Po polonium [209]	85 At astatine [210]	86 Rn radon [222]
87 Fr francium [223]	88 Ra radium [226]	89–103	104 Rf rutherfordium [261]	105 Db dubnium [262]	106 Sg seaborgium [266]	107 Bh bohrium [264]	108 Hs hassium [277]	109 Mt meitnerium [268]	110 Ds darmstadtium [271]	111 Rg roentgenium [272]	112 Cn copernicium [277]	113 Uut ununtrium unknown	114 Fl flerovium [289]	115 Uup ununpentium unknown	116 Lv livermorium [298]	117 Uus ununseptium unknown	118 Uuo ununoctium unknown

57 La lanthanum 138.91	58 Ce cerium 140.12	59 Pr praseodymium 140.91	60 Nd neodymium 144.24	61 Pm promethium [145]	62 Sm samarium 150.36	63 Eu europium 151.96	64 Gd gadolinium 157.25	65 Tb terbium 158.93	66 Dy dysprosium 162.50	67 Ho holmium 164.93	68 Er erbium 167.26	69 Tm thulium 168.93	70 Yb ytterbium 173.05	71 Lu lutetium 174.97
89 Ac actinium [227]	90 Th thorium 232.04	91 Pa protactinium 231.04	92 U uranium 238.03	93 Np neptunium [237]	94 Pu plutonium [244]	95 Am americium [243]	96 Cm curium [247]	97 Bk berkelium [247]	98 Cf californium [251]	99 Es einsteinium [252]	100 Fm fermium [257]	101 Md mendelevium [258]	102 No nobelium [259]	103 Lr lawrencium [262]

Legend:
- Alkali Metals
- Alkaline Earth Metals
- Transitional Metals
- Other Metals
- Metalloids
- Non-metals
- Noble Gases

INDEX

A

acid rain, vii, 88
acids, vii, 82–89
activities (Inquire & Investigate)
    Acid or Base? 89
    Boiling Point of Water, 46
    Build a Homemade
        Battery, 109
    Calculating Molar Mass, 80
    Converting Units, 8–10
    Creating a Fission
        Model, 98–99
    Element, Compound, or
        Mixture? 60–61
    Explore Evaporation and
        Condensation, 45
    Foaming Chemical
        Reactions, 78–79
    Identify Metal Ions With
        a Flame Test, 38
    Measuring Mass, 34–35
    Separating Mixtures with
        Chromatography, 62–63
    Three-Dimensional Atom, 21
    Using Density to Identify
        Unknown Metals, 36–37
    Using the Periodic Table, 22
allotropes, 26
alloys, 63
alpha decay, 94
anions, 13, 50–53, 104
anodes, 103–104
Aristotle, vi
Arrhenius, Svante, 83–84
atoms, vi–vii, 3, 12–22, 24–25,
    38, 40–41, 48–55, 58–59,
    67–71, 72, 75, 80, 82–89,
    92–99, 102–107
Avogadro's hypothesis, vi, 32–33

B

bases, 82–89
beta decay, 94–95
binding energy, 95
biochemistry, 107–108
Black, Joseph, vi
Bohr, Niels, vii
boiling point, 27, 42, 46, 52, 54
Boyle's law, vi, 30
Bronsted, Johannes, 84
buffers, 87

C

catalysts, 74, 75, 78–79, 108
cathodes, 103–104
cations, 13, 50–53, 72, 104
Chadwick, James, vii
Charles's law, 31
chemical equations, 69–71,
    73, 74, 94, 96
chemical reactions. (see also
    nuclear reactions)
    catalysts in, 74, 75, 78–79, 108
    chemical equations for,
        69–71, 73, 74
    definition and description
        of, 66–67
    electrochemistry study
        of, 102–104, 109
    equilibrium in, vi, 76–77
    half-life of, 97
    mole/molar mass
        measurements in,
        72–73, 74, 80
    percent composition
        calculation for, 80
    percent yield calculation for, 73
    rate of, 74–75
    reactants and products in,
        67–68, 69–71, 73–76, 78–79
    reverse/reversible, 76
    signs of, 68–69
    stoichiometry for, 73–74
    types of, 72
chemistry
    acids and bases in, vii, 82–89
    branches of, 102–109
    combinations in (see chemical
        reactions; compounds;
        mixtures; solutions)
    definition and description
        of, 2–4
    matter studied in (see matter)
    measurements in (see
        measurements)
    nuclear reactions in, vii, 92–99
    timeline of, vi–vii
coefficients, 70–71
colloids, 61
color, 38, 69, 87, 89
combined gas law, 32
combustion reactions, 72
compounds, vii, 50–55,
    60–61, 72, 105–107
concentration, 57, 75,
    76–77, 86, 88
condensation, 43, 45
covalent bonds/compounds,
    49–50, 53–55, 58, 105–106
crystals, 25, 26, 43, 52
Curie, Marie and Pierre, vii

D

Dalton, John, vi
decomposition reactions, 72
Democritus, vi
density, 36–37
deposition, 44
dilution, 57
dissolving, 59
dry ice, 44

E

Einstein, Albert, 96
electrochemistry, 102–104, 109
electrolytes, 51, 52–53,
    103–104, 109

electrons, vii, 12–21, 38, 49–55, 58–59, 83, 92, 94–95, 103–106
elements, vi–vii, 12, 15–20, 22, 26, 48, 50, 55, 60–61, 72, 80, 92–99, 103, 105–107
endothermic reactions, 72
energy, 4, 29, 38, 40–43, 69, 72, 74–75, 93, 95, 96–99, 102, 109 (*see also* electrons)
environmental issues, vii, 4, 88, 108
equilibrium, vi, 76–77
evaporation, 40, 42, 45
exothermic reactions, 72
experimental errors, 32, 37, 73

F

fission/fusion, nuclear, vii, 96–97, 98–99
freezing point, 43, 44
frost, 44

G

gamma decay/gamma rays, 95
gases, vi, 3, 24, 28–33, 40, 42–46, 68, 69–70, 106
Gay-Lussac's law, vi, 31
Geiger, Hans, vii
gravity, 34

H

Hahn, Otto, vii
half-life, 97

I

ideal gas law, 31
indicators, 87, 89
inhibitors, 75
insulators, 55
intermolecular forces, 27
ionic bonds/compounds, 49–53, 55, 72, 103

ions, 13, 38, 49–53, 55, 59, 72, 75, 82–89, 102–104
isotopes, vii, 18, 19–20, 93–94, 97

K

key questions, 7, 20, 33, 44, 59, 77, 88, 97, 108
kinetic energy, 29, 40–43, 69, 74–75
kinetic molecular theory of gases, 24, 29

L

Lavoisier, Antoine Laurent, vi
Le Chatelier, Henri/ Le Chatelier's principle, vi, 77
Libby, Willard, vii
liquids, 3, 24, 26–27, 28, 40, 41–46, 56–59, 69–70, 107
litmus testing, 87, 89
Loschmidt, Johann Josef, vi
Lowry, Thomas, 84

M

Marsden, Ernest, vii
mass, 34–35, 37, 40, 95, 96
mass defect, 95
matter
    building blocks of (*see* atoms; elements; molecules)
    changing states of, 40–46, 50
    combinations of (*see* chemical reactions; compounds; mixtures; solutions)
    definition of, 2, 3
    measurements of (*see* measurements)
    states of, vi, 3, 24–38, 40–46, 50 (*see also* gases; liquids; solids)

measurements
    accuracy of, 3, 43
    atomic mass, 16, 18, 19, 80
    converting units in, 8–10, 74
    density, 36–37
    mass, 34–35, 95
    metric system for, 4–5, 8–10, 34
    mole/molar mass, vi, 72–73, 74, 80
    percent composition calculation, 80
    percent yield calculation, 73
    precision of, 43
    pressure, 28
    scientific notation in, 67
    significant figures in, 6–7, 32
    temperature, 40
melting point, 27, 41, 52, 54
Mendeleev, Dmitri, vi, 16
metals, nonmetals, metalloids, 18–19, 36–38, 63, 104
Millikan, Robert, vii
mixtures, 55–56, 60–63 (*see also* solutions)
molecules, 3, 24–38, 40–44, 48–50, 54–59, 69–73, 75–77, 82–89, 106
mole/molar mass, vi, 72–73, 74, 80

N

names, of compounds, 53, 54
neutrons, vii, 12, 13, 19–20, 21, 92–99
nuclear reactions, vii, 92–99

O

ocean, pH of, 85
octet rule, 20
organic chemistry/synthesis, vi–vii, 105–107
oxidation state, 102–103

INDEX

P

Pauling, Linus, vii
percent composition calculation, 80
percent yield calculation, 73
periodic table, vi, 16–19,
    22, 50–51, 117
pH scale, vii, 85, 86–87
polar/nonpolar molecules,
    56, 58, 59
polyatomic ions, 52
potential energy, 69
precipitates, 69, 76, 77
pressure, vi, 28, 30–33, 41,
    42, 44, 46, 57–58, 77
Priestley, Joseph, vi
products, 67–68, 69–71,
    73–76, 78–79
protons, 12–13, 16, 19–20, 21,
    50–51, 83–85, 92–99

R

radioactivity, vii, 92–99
random error, 32, 37
reactants, 67–68, 69–71,
    73–76, 78–79
redox reactions, 103–104
Rutherford, Ernest, vii

S

scientific method, 10
scientific notation, 67
self-ionization, 82–83
Soddy, Frederick, vii
solids, 3, 24, 25, 28, 40, 41,
    43–44, 56, 69–70, 77
solubility, 58, 106
solutions, 46, 56–59,
    61, 82–89, 106
Sorensen, S.P.L., vii
Stahl, Georg, vi
static electricity, 13
stoichiometry, 73–74
strength, 85–86
sublimation, 44
surface tension, 27
suspensions, 57
synthesis reactions, 72
systematic error, 32, 37

T

temperature, 29, 30, 31–33,
    38, 40–46, 50, 57–58,
    69, 72, 75, 77, 106
Thomson, J.J., vii
timeline, vi–vii
titration, 88

V

valence electrons, 17, 18, 20, 105
vapor pressure, 42, 46
volume, vi, 25, 26, 28,
    30–33, 37, 77

W

weight, vii, 34, 73
Wöhler, Friedrich, vi, 106
Woodward, Robert, vii